Mary Ann or Ginger

The Dilemma in Every Man's Life and How to Deal With It

Barry Rothman

iUniverse, Inc.
New York   Bloomington

iUniverse books may be ordered through booksellers or by contacting:

iUniverse
1663 Liberty Drive
Bloomington, IN 47403
www.iuniverse.com
1-800-Authors (1-800-288-4677)

ISBN: 978-1-4401-4572-8 (sc)
ISBN: 978-1-4401-4573-5 (ebook)

Printed in the United States of America

iUniverse rev. date: 06/25/2009

This book is dedicated to my parents, the late Charles Rothman and Alice Rothman, who were happily married for fifty-eight years—they must have done something right; to my sister and brother-in-law, Janet and Jeff Ware—who also must be doing something right; to Elise Dickerson, my surrogate mom, office manager extraordinaire, and all-around factotum; to Sondra Locke for her friendship and encouragement and for suggesting that I write this book in the first place; and finally, in fond memory of my late, beloved dog, Zorro, for sitting in bed with me as I was attempting to compose this opus. I miss you so very much.

Contents

Introduction: The Conundrum   xi

   Mary Ann vs. Ginger or Tonya vs. Lara   xi

1. Groucho, the Little Tramp, and Me   1

2. The Best Years of Our Lives   5

3. Memories of Me   7

4. The Child   11

   First and Second Grade: Kathy the Storm Trooper 11

   Third Grade: Barry the Two-Timer (Wendy and
      Celia)   13

   Fourth Grade: Another Two-Girl Year and No
      Lessons Learned (Linda and Kathy)   14

   Fifth Grade: Diane the Two-Timer   15

   Sixth Grade: Robin the Goth— an Early Version
      of Avril Lavigne   16

   Seventh Grade: Barry Loses His Groove   17

   Eighth Grade: Cindy the *Shiksa* and My Bar
      Mitzvah   18

   Heidi the Drum Majorette   21

5. The Adolescent   23

Ninth Grade: Joani the Non-Virgin   23

Bonnie and the Imaginary Camera   25

Tenth Grade: Shari the Friend   26

Eleventh Grade: Jill the Body Beautiful   27

Twelfth Grade: Roslyn the Heartbreaker   28

6. The College Boy   31

Sophomore to Senior Year: Stacey the Model   31

Law School: Rhonda, My Very Own Laura Bush   34

7. The Man   37

Gayle: The Nonstop Talker   37

Jodi: The Live-in Lover   38

Melissa: The First Ballet Dancer   40

Sachi: From France Nuyen to Yoko Ono   41

Michelle: The Rich Taiwanese Virgin   43

Marcy: The Artistic Street Urchin   44

Li (meaning "beautiful"): The Chinese Princess   48

Alina: The Second Ballet Dancer   50

Barry: Licking My Wounds   54

Emily: The Exotic Dancer   54

Olga: The Last, and Certainly Least, Ballet Dancer   56

Kelly: The Felon   58

8. The Good, the Bad, and the Miscellaneous   61

Brenda: The Hawaiian Affair   61

The Hispanic Telemarketer   63

Elizabeth: The Drinker   64

Sandy: The Receptionist   66

Lera: The Office Manager and the Chinese Fire
    Drill   67

Angelina: The Hair Stylist   69

Jennifer: The Vamp   70

Audrey: The Teutonic Beauty   71

Ariane: The French Client   73

Jodi and the Bahamian Bodybuilder   73

Pam: The Temple and the Police   75

Diana: The Giantess   77

9. Foreign Affairs   79

Spartacus: The Matchmaker   79

Dr. Cathy: Thailand and the Scottish Doctor   80

Jo: Tasmania and the Aussie Dancer   84

Vanda: San Diego and the Russian Model   87

Montreal and the Nameless Indonesian Girl   89

Alexandra Hartman: The Aussie Girl Who Did
    Not Exist   90

10. Match.com and Other Disasters   93

Diane and the Car Door   94

Joan and Her CDs   94

Rachel the Stripper   95

Sunny, Kim, and the Korean Switch   96

Lisa, a.k.a. Hulk Hogan   96

Dana and Talking Dirty   97
Cynthia the Fashion Disaster   97
Kristi the Swing Dancer   98
Lydia the Aussie "Hottie"   98
Ashley and the Doggy Bag   99
Olga and Her Cell Phone   99
Katherine and *Her* Cell Phone   100
Kristen the Talker   100
Svetlana and the Kisses   101
Kate the Opera Singer   101

11. Dating Services That I Have Known   103
Great Expectations   103
It's Just Lunch   103
Eight Minute Dating   104
eHarmony   104
Match.com   105
Meetup.com   105
Cherry Blossoms   106
Anastasia   106

12. Some Conclusions on Life, Liberty, and the Pursuit of Women   109

Postscript   115

Introduction: THE CONUNDRUM

Mary Ann vs. Ginger

or

Tonya vs. Lara

This choice, my friends, is an important fork in the road for all boys on their way to manhood, or for all men on their way back to boyhood.

As a boy, I never recognized the beauty of the actresses that I saw on television in programs such as *Bewitched*, *I Dream of Jeannie*, *Get Smart*, or even *Leave It to Beaver*. ("What a beautiful dress you have on, Mrs. Cleaver.") In fact, I didn't even think of Elizabeth Montgomery, Barbara Eden, Barbara Feldon, or other similar actresses as attractive girls or women or anything other than characters on TV. Now that I look back on it, I can appreciate the charms of those actresses. They were all quite beautiful women—although I really think that one of the key signs of aging is when you start thinking that June Cleaver (Barbara Billingsley) is actually hot. I even watched *Petticoat Junction*, but again, the charms of those young actresses as well as the true meaning behind the fictional name of Hooterville completely escaped me.

And then there was *Gilligan's Island*, one of my favorite TV shows as a young boy. Give me a break, I was only ten years old. Now when I see pictures of Dawn Wells as Mary Ann, I think, "My God, she was gorgeous!" But at the time, dear, sweet, and kind Mary Ann made about as much an impression on me as Gilligan or Mrs. Howell. And before you ask, I still do not view Mrs. Howell as a babe—you smart aleck! No, it was Ginger (Tina Louise), the sexy, conniving bad girl who made the greatest impression on me. Even at that young age, I thought she was hot. Every time she attempted to seduce Gilligan, I was a goner. Why? I don't know. Maybe I was genetically predisposed to like the bad girl. Maybe I still am.

Then, when I was eleven years old, my parents took me to see my first grown-up movie, *Doctor Zhivago*—another crossroads.

For those of you who haven't seen the movie, it revolves around a young poet and doctor, Yuri (Omar Sharif), his beautiful wife, Tonya (Geraldine Chaplin), and his mistress, the perfect-looking—and I do mean perfect-looking—siren, Lara (Julie Christie).

I really didn't understand the movie very well. The Bolsheviks, the Tsar, the Russian Revolution, and so on were way above my head at the time. But what was clear to me was the life choice Yuri had to make with respect to his love life. Should he stay with Tonya, be surrounded by a loving and wealthy family, have a beautiful wife who adored him, and live out a peaceful life in Paris? Or should he pursue that gorgeous temptress Lara, enjoy brief moments of exquisite bliss, and end up acting out the best death scene in movie history—prematurely aged, clutching his heart, and falling to the ground next to a tram on a lonely Moscow street? For all you movie buffs, the second best death scene in movie history is, in my humble opinion, that of David McCallum in *The Great Escape*, but I digress.

If you have ever seen *Dr. Zhivago*, you will recall the scene where Lara is about to go to a party with the villainous character played by Rod Steiger. There is a shot in that scene of Lara dressed up in a gorgeous red gown looking into a mirror. At that point in time and in that scene, Christie was, without a doubt, the most beautiful woman in the world—a modern Helen of Troy. That scene is indelibly etched into my memory.

In any event, the choice between Mary Ann and Ginger or between Tonya and Lara is the choice we boys or men all face, if indeed we have the good fortune to face such a choice at all. As for me, I regrettably have chosen the path leading to Ginger and Lara, and ultimately, disappointment, sadness, and regret. Trust me, I will be avoiding Moscow trams for the foreseeable future. I don't want to tempt fate.

For this purpose, forget about all those music boxes playing "Lara's Theme." Every time I hear one, I want Yuri to run right back into Tonya's arms, or, alternatively, I want to smash the box into a hundred pieces. Does anyone really buy those things? When I was in Switzerland, I could not pass a store without seeing and/or hearing one. "Somewhere my love ..." But I digress again.

Speaking of choices, I have great stories to tell the grandkids about life and love, but one needs to be able to get a date on Saturday night before grandchildren enter into the picture. In any event, please read on and let me know if I have made any of the right choices.

Chapter One: Groucho, the Little Tramp, and Me

Many years ago, Groucho Marx wrote a book called *Memoirs of a Mangy Lover*. I love that title. (It is even better than Fred Allen's *Much Ado About Me*.) In his book, Groucho's described his many romantic adventures. Unfortunately for him, the book was complete fiction, and to Groucho's everlasting chagrin, it was his brother, Chico, who always "got the girls" (as they romantically described it in those days).

Chico (pronounced "Chicko," as it was originally spelled) got his nickname, as he was a "chick chaser." He was not just a chaser. He apparently caught them all. You can see his charisma as he flirts with beautiful, blonde Thelma Todd in the Marx Brothers' movie *Horse Feathers*. There is no denying it. (Poor Thelma was rubbed out by the mob shortly thereafter; sad, but true.) There is even a rumor that a much older Chico bedded a much younger Marilyn Monroe when Marilyn had a bit part in the last Marx Brothers' movie, *Love Happy*. I wonder if it really happened. If so, what could she have been thinking? Career advancement, no doubt. By the way, apparently Harpo did all right with the women as well. He never caught them in the movies, but did so quite often in real life. Poor Groucho was apparently the runt of the Marx litter.

1

By the way, I will use the term "girls" often, as I still tend to think in terms of "guys" and "girls" (but, not "guys" and "dolls"—definitely not one of my favorite musicals, by the way), but I will use the term interchangeably with "women." Just thought you'd like to know there is nothing sexist about it—at least I hope not.

In these memoirs (unlike Groucho's *Memoirs*), you will hear the truth, the whole truth, and nothing but the truth. After all, I am an attorney. All right, no snide comments. Also, the names will not be changed, as there are no innocents to protect. Well, maybe some of the names will be changed to protect me—from lawsuits, that is.

Just so you know, I have been compared in looks by many people to the actor Kyle MacLachlan, but truthfully, I don't see it. He is taller, and I am better looking (he says sheepishly). But then again, you don't see me on *Desperate Housewives*. Damn! But I guess that looking like Kyle MacLachlan is better than looking like Victor McLaglen. (All you old movie buffs will understand—for the rest of you, there is Google.)

I have been actively dating since 1960. Yes, I was six years old and in the first grade. Actually, I did have a crush on someone in kindergarten named Debbie, but that doesn't count, as I was too young and immature at the time. However, I did kiss her hand in the coatroom one day, resulting in a scandal in our kindergarten class. I was advanced for my age—at least I thought so.

I am not sure that I will be able to provide any profound advice to readers of this book, but by reading of my many relationships and romantic adventures, you may avoid the mistakes that I have made, and maybe even copy the one or two things that I have done right over the years. As I am still single and without children at this late date, you will have to determine for yourself whether or not I have done anything right at all.

But then again, I look to Anthony Quinn and Tony Randall, two men who had children in their dotage. Unfortunately, they are no longer around to see their children grow up. And then there is, of course, Charlie Chaplin, my hero for all sorts of reasons, some even admirable.

Chaplin loved much younger women (girls?) and suffered both legally, financially, and otherwise for his interest (fetish?). By the way, I think they called such girls "San Quentin quail" back in the day. Cute, huh? Anyway, good old Charlie had a habit of dating and/or marrying teenage girls. And then in his fifties, Chaplin married gorgeous eighteen-year-old Oona O'Neill (the daughter of playwright Eugene O'Neill and the Paris Hilton of the 1940s). By the way, he fathered his last child with Oona in his early seventies. Go, Little Tramp, go.

Chaplin was a cinematic genius, of course, and he suffered in many ways for his relationships and/or marriages to much younger women. But in the end, he appeared to have a large and happy family life and to have found the peace that had eluded him earlier in his life. This is my way of saying that there is always hope, or at least I hope so.

As an aside, Emily Dickinson wrote, in her poem "Hope" that "Hope is the thing with feathers that perches in the soul ..." I love that poem and have read it a hundred times. I just wish that I knew what it meant. Oh well. I will just have to keep reading it.

Chapter Two: The Best Years Of Our Lives

As you have probably already surmised, I love old movies. One of my favorite American movies of all time is William Wyler's post-war *The Best Years of Our Lives* (1946) starring Fredric March, Myrna Loy, Dana Andrews, Virginia Mayo (yum!), Teresa Wright, Harold Russell, and Cathy O'Donnell. Never seen it? Put it on your Netflix queue immediately.

The movie revolves around three servicemen in the aftermath of World War II returning to their fictional, all-American hometown, Boone City. Sergeant Al (March), an alcoholic banker, returns to his loving wife of twenty years, Milly (Loy). Bombardier Fred (Andrews) returns to his gorgeous, party-girl wife, Marie (Mayo—yum, again!), but later falls in love with Al's daughter, all-American girl, Peggy (Wright). Meanwhile, disabled vet Homer (Russell) returns, with hooks in place of his hands, to his next-door neighbor/fiancée, Wilma (O'Donnell). Did you get all that?

Was there ever really a town like Boone City? Was there ever really a perfect marriage like the one portrayed between Al and Milly? (Maybe not, as Loy herself was married five times.) Could a next-door romance really flourish between Homer and Wilma, especially after Homer's burnt hands were replaced by hooks? And could upper-class Peggy really have found true love with working-class Fred? I like to think so.

If I was Fred, I would, of course, have tried to salvage my marriage to Marie—what great legs! And that decision would seem to mirror almost all of my decisions concerning love and relationships: misguided and completely wrong. Did I already mention those great legs? Well ... at least I wasn't alone. For all of you trivia buffs, Mayo was just one of the many beautiful and anonymous 1940s Goldwyn Girls when Samuel Goldwyn plucked her out of obscurity and made her a star, all because of those great stems. But I digress ... once again and for the last time.

Chapter Three: Memories of Me

As we are still strangers, let me introduce myself. My name is Barry. I was born at Mount Sinai Hospital in Boone City ... hmm, I mean Cleveland, Ohio, on July 7, 1954. I share a birthday with Marc Chagall and Ringo Starr, but I do not share their artistic abilities (see below).

My paternal grandparents were from Russian stock. In fact, I do not even know if the family name was Rothman. I am quite sure it was something else, but the personnel at Ellis Island decided on Rothman—just like Vito Andolini became Vito Corleone in *The Godfather 2*. My maternal grandparents, the Wodickas, were originally from Bohemia (now the Czech Republic). In fact, I was able to trace the Wodicka clan back to Prague in the seventeen hundreds. Possibly, my Bohemian roots are to blame for some of my decision-making with respect to love.

I was born with a dislocated hip and was attended to by a specialist and innovator in the field of pediatric hip dislocations at the time, a Dr. Barry Friedman, hence my first name. My mom wanted to name me Robin but was afraid that I would be teased as "Robin Red-Breast" and all. Actually, I would have quite preferred the name Robin. It didn't seem to hurt Robin Williams. In any event, I had a rather *Leave It to Beaver*-type of existence, except that my mom did not wear pearls while she cleaned the house, and dad did not wear a suit and tie at the dinner table.

My sister, Janet, was, and still is, two years older than me. And we were, and still are, very close. One of my earliest memories was of a severe snowstorm in Cleveland. I was about three years old, and the snow was over my head, but my sister cleared a path in the snow so that I could actually move up and down the street. That was awfully nice of her. Someday I should thank her. Maybe I just did.

When I was nine years old, we moved to Dallas, Texas—a small, sleepy Texas town at the time, if you can believe it. This move was two months before President Kennedy was assassinated. I had nothing to do with it, I swear. However, I did carpool to elementary school every day with Jack Ruby's nephews, Brian and Fred. It's true. They were both very nice boys. After the assassination, they quietly moved back to Chicago, for you see, Dallas seemed to hate Ruby even more than it hated Lee Harvey Oswald. Could it have been because Ruby was Jewish? That was what my parents thought at the time. As I stated, Dallas was a very different city back then. For example, I was a big wrestling fan as a youngster, and two of the most popular wrestlers in the Dallas area at that time were Fritz Von Erich—complete with Nazi regalia, and Killer Karl Kox—with KKK stenciled on his boots. Never would this happen in today's Dallas, or anywhere else, thank God. In any event, once the Ruby children moved away, my brush with infamy came to an end. I wonder whatever became of them.

My school years were happy ones, for the most part, with no great traumas. I was not the most popular kid in class, but I was pretty popular and had many friends of both sexes throughout my school career. I was a cheerleader finalist in high school, but did not get enough votes to become a cheerleader—sad, but not disastrous. But that event kind of mirrored my school social life— not the most popular, but certainly not the least popular. After graduation from high school, I spent one year at the University of Texas in Austin as a sad and lonely freshman. Then, deciding that I needed to get the hell out of Texas, I spent three years at the University of Colorado in Boulder, where I graduated with a Bachelor's degree in business finance. Then I went back to Dallas for two years of law school at Southern Methodist University (back to Texas—what was I thinking?). I finally finished up law school at the University of Denver, where I received my Juris Doctor (law degree). I had a love-hate relationship with Texas. Can you tell?

Although I am an attorney, I've always had a love for the fine arts—art, music, acting, dance, etc., and I have tried my hand at most of these pursuits. I took lessons and played—or attempted to play—the piano, clarinet, flute, and guitar. I actually played the clarinet in the school band for six years. Much later, I did some acting locally, was a member of the Screen Actor's Guild for three years, and had a memorable (?) performance in a Perry Mason made-for-television movie, *The Case of the Scandalous Scoundrel.* It lasted all of ten seconds, but I was so proud. After the episode ended, I called my parents and asked them what they thought. They said, "Were you in it? We must have missed you." Barry, be not proud. I also acted in some local television commercials. Finally, I did some print ad model work, where I was a bit more successful, appearing in a number of newspaper advertisements.

Later, I took ballet, jazz, and swing dance lessons,

even appearing in a local production of *The Nutcracker*. I remember one of my ballet teachers always screaming at me, "Barry, your *other* left foot!" Do you remember the hippos performing ballet in tutus in the Disney movie *Fantasia*? Similarities abound. But I had fun and was able to meet a number of ballet dancers, some of whom you will meet in the following chapters.

I preferred ballet dancers to lawyers, but ultimately, I stuck with the law. I have often been asked why I became a lawyer. The answer that always comes to mind is that I did so because I cannot play the flute like Sir James Galway. I think that that is a truthful answer, but don't get me wrong: I do enjoy the practice of law, as I enjoy teaching and helping people. At least that aspect of the practice of law is satisfying to me. The nicest compliment that I ever received from a client was that, for an attorney, I had a wonderful bedside manner. And I think that that assessment is quite accurate.

After almost thirty years of law practice in Denver, I decided to shake things up and move to my favorite city in the United States, San Diego. (Paris remains my favorite city in the world. *Mais oui!*) And so, here I am in San Diego to begin my search for a woman, a satisfying career, a woman, etc. You get the picture.

One more thing. There is a French proverb, which goes something like this: "In love, there is always the one who kisses and the one who offers the cheek." I have always been the kisser/suitor. Maybe it is a function of being a male, or maybe not. But that aspect of my character may explain some of the incidents connected to the relationships described in the following chapters. And just in case you are wondering, I am still "always the one who kisses."

Chapter Four: The Child

First and Second Grade: Kathy the Storm Trooper

I always enjoyed the first week of school each new school year for the very specific reason that I got to scout out the new girls in my class. Very exciting, those first few days of school! As a schoolboy, I would always differentiate the girls in my class between girls you noticed the first day (gorgeous), girls you noticed the second day (very attractive), and, girls you noticed the third day (attractive). I didn't always fall for first-day girls, but invariably, I would fall for first-, second-, or third-day girls.

My first relationship lasted two years—pretty good for a first-grader. Her name was Kathy. She had short blonde hair, big blue eyes, and a cute button nose. She reminds me now of a very young, much cuter version of Hillary Clinton, if such a thing is possible. Unfortunately, sometime during our two years together, she informed me that her parents "hated Jews." *Oy vey!* (Or, *oy gevalt,* if you prefer.) I had never encountered anti-Semitism before. What was that all about?

My parents grew up as American Jews during World War II, and apparently, they used to speculate about which gentile (non-Jewish) families among their friends would hide them if Hitler ever came to power in the

11

United States. I am sure that many American Jews were similarly traumatized during the war, especially given the ferocious nature of the German war machine. Either they would have had to start speaking German or end up as lampshades, according to Michael Weiner, a.k.a. Michael Savage of *The Savage Nation*. Even after the war and my birth, my parents would still evaluate their gentile friends on that basis. Strange, but true.

I grew up in a mixed ethnic neighborhood with mostly Italian-Americans as my neighbors. I learned early on that my next-door neighbors, the Denallos, would probably hide us from the Nazis, but my across-the-street neighbors, the Salvatores, probably would not hide us. In fact, not only would they probably not hide us, but they would also betray us in the event that they knew where we were hiding. Quite heady stuff for a six-year-old.

In any event, given all that information, the relationship with Kathy had to end. She may not have been a storm trooper, but she was certainly no Miep Gies. (Gies was the woman who helped to hide Anne Frank and her family from the Nazis during World War II. As of this writing, she has reached the age of one hundred years old. Good karma.) I can hear the storm-trooper boots as I write this. Poor Kathy, she probably didn't even realize what she was saying. But I can't make that same excuse for her parents, who should have known better.

Conclusion: What conclusions can anyone draw from a first and second grade romance? Well, a flip answer would be that one should never date a Nazi, but a more serious and reflective answer would paraphrase John Lennon's song "Revolution"—don't surround yourself with people with minds that hate. I guess that advice is good, no matter how old you are.

Third Grade: Barry the Two-Timer
(Wendy and Celia)

Third grade was a successful year for me. My regular-school girlfriend was Wendy, a dazzling brunette with a great smile and beautiful brown eyes. My Sunday-school girlfriend was Celia, a girl with two big brown pigtails and two missing front teeth. That look actually passed for beauty in the third grade. The year was fairly uneventful, but happily busy with two girlfriends. It never even occurred to me that I was a two-timer. Didn't everyone have a regular-school girlfriend and a Sunday-school girlfriend? Maybe not.

Truthfully, I do harbor one regret. A year later, after I had moved to Dallas, I returned to Cleveland to visit my old school chums. However, when I saw Wendy approach, I literally ran away from her and never saw her again. Why did I run? Why didn't I stay and talk to her? I don't know. Later, I was ashamed and disappointed in myself. Still am.

Conclusion: It is never too early to learn good lessons. I should have taken myself over my knee and given myself a good spanking. (A neat trick if it could be done—you try it.) I should also have told myself that one girlfriend at a time was enough for anyone—I think that should be the case for a third-grader or anyone else. Two-timing is never a good idea. Unfortunately, I would disregard that advice many times in the future.

Fourth Grade: Another Two-Girl Year
and No Lessons Learned
(Linda and Kathy)

Who would have guessed that "the future" would begin the next year, in fourth grade?

This time we were all in the same class at regular school—a potentially more combustible situation. The two girls were Linda and Kathy. Linda was a very sexy (for fourth grade) brunette with a knowing smile, a twinkle in her eyes, and a cute, dimpled chin. Linda was quite advanced for her age and wanted to "make out." I didn't even know exactly what that term meant at the time. She was adorable, and I was scared to death of her. One time she came at me with open arms, wanting to kiss me. I actually fled in terror. No Cary Grant here.

Kathy was a cute, brunette, chipmunk-cheeked girl with flashing dark eyes who became a real beauty in high school. Had I known, I would have waited for her.

All of us immature fourth-grade boys used to knock Kathy's pencils off her desk so we could sneak a peek when she bent down to pick them up. ("I see London; I see France …") Shameful. Homer Simpson would have been proud.

To this day, I never learned whether or not they knew about each other. They must have. Maybe they didn't care, or maybe they were "seeing others," as well. I use that term rather loosely. Remember, this is fourth grade we are talking about.

But with the school year ending, there was summertime with the boys, and the hope of a new romance in the new school year.

Conclusion: See third grade above—same conclusion, which reminds me of a scene in The Marx Brothers' movie, *Duck Soup*. Margaret Dumont to Groucho: "This is a gala day for you." Of course, Groucho replies to Margaret Dumont: "That's good. I don't think I could handle more than a gal a day." Well ... it was funny when *he* said it.

Fifth Grade: Diane the Two-Timer

Okay, I'll say it before you do: What goes around, comes around. Or, what's good for the goose is good for the gander, I might add, especially as it concerns affairs of the heart. This was the year that Barry got his comeuppance. (I think that I learned this word by reading the stories about young Henry Huggins by Beverly Cleary, which I loved.)

Diane was simply the best-looking girl in the fifth grade. She had beautiful blonde hair, blue eyes, a dazzling smile, and dark eyebrows. (I've always liked the combination of blonde hair and dark eyebrows.) Picture a young Cameron Diaz—oh my. I spent almost all of fifth grade thinking that we were in an exclusive relationship—again, if one can actually be in an exclusive relationship in fifth grade. We never saw each other outside of school. In fact, I don't think we even talked on the phone. But I felt secure in our "relationship." Unfortunately, Diane moved away at the end of that class year. It was only then that I learned that she had had a second boyfriend. You guessed it, it was one of my best friends, Mitch.

I was beside myself. I was a handsome young boy. Mitch was tall, awkward, and hardly attractive. How could this be? Could Diane have been interested in facets of Mitch other than his less than ordinary looks? Could there be interesting things about the opposite sex other than good looks? Did I have so much to learn about these things? Could I learn them or would I be mentally stuck in fifth grade for all time?

Conclusion: I think that I can now finally answer all of the questions in the prior paragraph. And I think that I may actually be able to answer most of them correctly. You try answering them and see how you do. Then draw your own conclusions. (You didn't think there would be a pop quiz, did you?)

Sixth Grade: Robin the Goth— an Early Version of Avril Lavigne

Her name was Robin, and we were *the* couple of the sixth grade. We were the Tom Cruise/Katie Holmes of Preston Hollow Elementary School—the talk of the sixth grade. I kind of liked that. She looked like a sixth-grade version of the young Avril Lavigne (kind of Goth, very pretty), and I was in love. You will note that none of the girls, past or present, will seem to have much in common except that I thought that they were adorable. Is this a bad portent for the future?

In any event, this was love. Robin and I always stared at each other in class, passed notes to each other, ate lunch together, and did all the other things that sixth graders do. I believe that I even once kissed her on the cheek. In fact, I know that I kissed her on the cheek more than once. Move over, Errol Flynn.

Robin moved out of state during the middle of the school year, and I found myself without a girlfriend for the first time since first grade. I was crushed. Why?

Because Robin moved away or because I was left without a girlfriend? When you figure that one out, please let me know. I like to think that I matured during that time period, but as subsequent events will show, I may be mistaken in that assumption.

Conclusion: I don't have one. Maybe, had Robin stuck around the whole school year, I would have had something to conclude about. You may conclude, then, that I was still clueless.

Seventh Grade: Barry Loses His Groove

Oh my God! Could I have lost my groove (or my "mojo" as Austin Powers might say) so soon? I fell in love with, in consecutive order, Lucille, Mary Ann (no, not Gilligan's Mary Ann), Ellen, and Linda. And … nothing. What could I be doing wrong? As it turns out, I still don't know. I do know that it was a frustrating year. Unfortunately, I would continue to relive the failures of seventh grade from time to time as I got older.

Speaking of Linda, did you ever know a girl in school who you were in love with for years, and that love remained unrequited? For me, that girl was Linda. I met her in seventh grade and was in love with her from the first time I saw her, through high school graduation. We were friends, but I was never able to switch gears from platonic friendship to romance. All the while I watched her go from one romantic relationship to the next with an endless series of losers. No, I'm not bitter, just honest. Even many years later, at the few high school reunions that I attended, I always kept an eagle-eye out for Linda, but I never saw her again.

My reflections on my past failures (a very painful subject) would not be complete without including all women named Rachel or Sara. I have fallen for many women over the years whose names were either Rachel or Sara. And I have never, ever been successful at establishing a relationship with someone of either name. I can't explain it. Something biblical, I presume.

Yes, it is always the ones that get away that you think about the most. Ask any fishing enthusiast.

Conclusion: I can just hear Dr. Phil telling me in his distinctive Texas drawl that "It is okay to be alone." And I think that he would probably be right. But believing it and living it are two separate and distinct things. Whenever I am alone, I always feel like it would be better to be with someone. And many times, when I am with someone, I feel like it would be better to be alone. There you have the definition of a bachelor.

Speaking of Dr. Phil, have you ever thought that you needed analysis twenty-four hours a day? Well, sometimes I envision Dr. Phil following me around, all day and every day, vigorously scribbling in his notepad. Maybe I don't need such analysis, but it couldn't hurt. Are you listening, Dr. Phil? I think I need a lifetime appointment.

Eighth Grade: Cindy the *Shiksa* and My Bar Mitzvah

Cindy was the first girl that I kissed on the lips. Wow, who invented that? I loved it. As George and Ira Gershwin wrote, "How long has this been going on?" (a brilliant song).

Cindy was an adorable blonde with black, horn-rimmed glasses, which only made her more adorable in my eyes. She was also the first girl that I dated who wore makeup. This made her very mature and a big turn-on, at least from an eighth-grader's point of view.

I remember distinctively my mother driving me to the movie theatre to meet Cindy for my "first date." The movie was *Snow White and the Seven Dwarfs.* I didn't care a thing about Snow White or her dwarfs. All I cared about was sitting in the back of the theater and making out with Cindy, to the great annoyance of everyone around us. But she was such a good kisser. Well ... I really had nothing to compare it to, so I can only assume she was a good kisser.

During that summer, I became a bar-mitzvah boy. Besides all the presents that I expected to receive, I was looking forward to "becoming a man." Wow. What was going to happen to me? Would I grow a beard? Would I become Charles Atlas? I knew nothing then, and perhaps very little even now, of testosterone.

Well, I made it through the religious ceremony, faking it all the way. I had not studied very well, so throughout much of the ceremony, I was just throwing out guttural sounds that sounded to me very Hebraic. I could just see poor Rabbi Klein rolling his eyes upward. Later, a non-Jewish friend of my dad's came up to me and told me that, although he didn't speak Hebrew, he could tell that I had really mastered it. At least I fooled someone. Okay, okay, back to Cindy.

After the religious part of the ceremony, I was supposed to be on hand for something called a cake-cutting ceremony. As I recall, that was where each member of the family would cut a piece of cake and do something with it. Who remembers? It was a long time ago. In any event, I was nowhere to be found, and a big search began for the bar-mitzvah boy. Finally, my best friend, David, bolted into the temple game room (yes, the temple had a game room) and found me lying on the pool table making out with Cindy. I was a man after all, wasn't I? I ran back just in time to cut the first slice of cake. Cindy joined me soon after.

It was at that time that "The Scandal" erupted. You see, Cindy was a *shiksa*. What is a *shiksa*? Many Jewish mothers would define the term as "a non-Jewish girl, God forbid." Cindy was not only a Christian, but, God forgive her, she also wore a prominent cross around her neck. The Jews in the room, who were, as you might imagine a majority, were outraged. How dare she wear a Christian cross to a Jewish bar mitzvah? I didn't care. Did I mention that she was a good kisser?

Cindy moved out of state shortly thereafter. I hope she did not leave with a bad impression of the Jewish people. Maybe just the Reform Jews of Dallas.

Conclusion: Well, I have no regrets about dating Cindy, taking her to the bar mitzvah, or making out in the game room. If I had it to do all over again, I would probably do it the same way, at least with respect to Cindy. But I would take my bar mitzvah a bit more seriously. I probably let a lot of people down that day. It's never too late. I read that Kirk Douglas (a devout Jew) had his second bar mitzvah at the age of eighty-three, as many devout Jews do. That will give me an extra thirty years or so to brush up on my Hebrew.

Heidi the Drum Majorette

Her name was Heidi. She was of German parentage, and she was the sexiest little blonde Aryan girl you could imagine. She was also a ninth-grader and was the head drum majorette in the Benjamin Franklin Junior High School marching band. I, on the other hand, was a not-too-geeky (I promise) eighth-grader who played (or attempted to play) the clarinet in the marching band. I had the biggest crush on her since—well, since forever.

We were friends, but even had she been romantically interested in me (which she was not), she was a year older than me, and no self-respecting ninth-grade girl would ever have a boyfriend who was a mere eighth-grader. I was still crazy about her.

It didn't help matters that I had to play the clarinet and march directly behind her. Let's see … on the one hand, I could pay attention to my marching and the music attached to the music stand on my clarinet. On the other hand, I could pay attention to Heidi's adorable backside dressed in her short, drum-majorette's skirt. Well, you now know why I never became the Benny Goodman of my generation.

Heidi moved away after that year. I stayed in the band one more year, but the thrill was gone, as Heidi's replacement was utterly forgettable. But I will never forget Heidi and the exquisite way in which she marched—unforgettable.

Conclusion: As Mick Jagger sang, "You can't always get what you want." I am not sure that he was referring to Heidi the drum majorette, but you never can tell. If he had only seen her. Yikes! The song continues (and I am paraphrasing), "but, if you try sometime, you just might find, you get what you need." Mick, I had been trying. I promise.

Chapter Five: The Adolescent

Ninth Grade: Joani the Non-Virgin

Even after my heavy-petting experience with Cindy, I was still a complete neophyte when it came to things sexual—that is, until I met Joani.

Joani said that she was no longer a virgin. I kind of knew what that meant, but the implications were completely lost to me. She sure did like to talk about her sexual past, probably just to get a rise out of me, either figuratively or literally, or both. In looking back on it, I think she was probably just as much a virgin as I was, but I was very gullible—still am.

Joani was from the other side of the tracks. I was from an upper-middle-class background, and she was from the lower classes. But she intrigued me, due in no small part I am sure, to the fact that she was light years ahead of me, sexually speaking.

She claimed to have something called "skin attacks," which meant she liked to take my shirt and pants off. Then what? I never figured it out, and if she had been as experienced as she claimed, she would have helped me to figure it out. By the way, these "skin attacks" did not go both ways. Joani never shed any clothes as I remember, and I think I would remember. But I went along with it.

Who wouldn't at that age, even if it was very embarrassing on those dates during which we were doubling.

Joani was also the first girl I encountered whose actions and personality scared me. She was extremely jealous. She called at least four or five times a day and was extremely moody. At the time, all I knew to do was to break up with her as a form of self-preservation. That aspect of her was quite scary, and I would experience it with other girls later on. I had a choice to make—put up with her antics in the hopes of more sexual experiences, or run away and run fast. I ran. ("Run, Forrest, run!")

Joani left my life as abruptly as she came into it (no pun intended). Even at that young age, I considered it a blessing. I hope she finally found peace and happiness.

On a lighter note, I was recently reminded of a funny story related to Joani. One day my friend, Bruce, Joani, and I were hanging out in my bedroom and were very bored. My sister had on her bookshelf *The Joy of Sex*, which was relatively new at the time. To this day, I still don't know how my parents allowed it. In any event, I got the book, Bruce read of the various sexual positions described, and Joani and I acted them out (fully clothed, mind you). The three of us thought it was hilarious. Well, my mother, who is generally very laid back, charged into my bedroom like a bull moose and told us to knock it off (in so many words). We did not feel that we had done anything wrong, but did as we were told. To make matters worse, I don't think that I learned anything. Damn.

Conclusion: I don't care whether you are in ninth grade or ninety years old: when you encounter someone with seeming personality disorders, run, don't walk, out of that relationship. This advice does not apply if you are in a committed relationship and your spouse begins exhibiting problems—I am not one to be speaking about that issue. But if it is a new relationship, watch out for warning signs, be aware, and be prepared to leave unless you want to devote your life to trying to help someone who may be beyond your help. Don't try to play Florence Nightingale or Mother Teresa—it's just not worth it.

Bonnie and the Imaginary Camera

Bonnie was simply the sexiest girl this ninth-grader had ever seen. Her skin, her eyes, her nose, her teeth, her figure, her legs ... you get the picture. We were in a few classes together and were platonic friends. Poor Plato—did he ever have any girlfriends? I haven't done my research, but I believe that young boys were his thing. To each his own.

In any event, in our classes together, I just could not stop staring at Bonnie. One day she finally said, "Take a picture, it will last longer." I didn't know what she meant. She explained it to me. I like to think that it cured me from further staring at her, but I don't think it did. In fact, I know that it did not.

Whatever happened to Bonnie? Well, I saw her at a high school reunion a number of years ago, and, bless her heart, she had turned into Rosemary Clooney or Stevie Nicks—she was as big as a tent. I felt terrible. For her or for me? I'm not sure, but I sure was sorry to see her that way. I hope she has had a nice life regardless of appearance. "The way we were." Indeed.

Conclusion: None really. Just a tinge of sadness. We all get older and some of us age better than others. It's called *life*.

Tenth Grade: Shari the Friend

Shari was probably the healthiest relationship of my life up until that time, which may not be saying much. She was a nice Jewish girl from down the street, whom I had known since elementary school. Somehow she had blossomed into a striking brunette, and I was smitten. It was such a nice relationship, as we were just very good friends who also were romantically interested in each other. Then somehow, for some reason, the relationship morphed back into a nice friendship. And that was just fine with me.

Later on, I acted as her "beard." Let me explain. Shari's parents were strict Orthodox Jews who did not allow her to date non-Jews. Oh, the intolerance of some people. Anyway, my best friend at the time, Rod, was very interested in Shari, and vice-versa. But, oh my God, he was a non-Jew. What to do? Well, I would pick her up, drive her to my house, transfer her to Rod's car, wait for them, transfer her back to my car, and take her home. It was all very altruistic of me. Rod and Shari dated for some time, but ultimately and much later, Shari married a well-connected, wealthy attorney who, of course, was Jewish. Her parents were thrilled. As I understand it, they still are.

On a side note, Shari's house always smelled like macaroni and cheese. I could never figure that one out. It's funny the things that we remember. Every time I think of Shari, I think of mac and cheese and vice-versa.

Conclusion: A wise old man once told me to marry your best friend. I would presume that he also meant that you should also date your best friend. I think that that is good advice. She may not be the best-looking girl, the most intelligent, or the best in bed (God forbid), but you will have an equal partner through life, and that ain't half-bad.

Eleventh Grade: Jill the Body Beautiful

As I look back on Jill (which is, in itself, a wonderful experience), I must admit that she had the greatest body of any girl I have dated, either before or since—and since I am a typically shallow male, I have dated many girls with exquisite figures. In any event, I was madly in love with Jill (or with Jill's body—you decide). However, my attempts at love-making, or at least making-out, were completely one-sided. She was one of those girls who would undress and allow you to do anything (within reason) to her body, but she absolutely refused to reciprocate. Did I care? You know the answer.

Jill lived in a scary old house and had a scary old mother. Think of the Addams Family house with a very ugly Morticia Addams ruling the roost. I would brave it and her mother and visit Jill at her home anyway. You can guess why. Jill lived far away, and I was not yet old enough for my driver's license, but with lust in my heart, I completely destroyed my favorite bicycle. Just think about it: I wore out my new bike in exchange for frequent encounters with Jill. Well, I guess that it was worth it.

One such visit is still ingrained in my memory. Jill had two (at least) boyfriends at the time, me and another whose name escapes me. Let's just call him the Jerk. No, I'm not a bitter person. Well, maybe just a little. Anyway, one night, both of us came to court her. She placed me in one room and the Jerk in another room. She would come to my room, kiss me, and tell me that she was trying to get rid of the Jerk. Then she would go to the other room containing the Jerk and tell him the same thing about me. We both knew what was going on, but our hormones were raging, and so we both stayed put … did I tell you about that body? Ultimately, she ended up with the Jerk.

After high school, I learned that she married the Jerk. No hard feelings. They were probably deserving of each other. I wonder if they are still married. And what has become of that body? Gravity, I suspect.

Conclusion: This is an easy one. Don't ever play the fool for anyone—especially if you know that you are doing so. Forget the girl, the body, and the sex (yes, all of those) and keep your self-respect. It is worth much more than all of those other things by at least a hundredfold. Trust me on this one. Also, your bicycle will last a lot longer.

Twelfth Grade: Roslyn the Heartbreaker

Roslyn was a "younger woman." I was a senior in high school, and she was a sophomore. Two years' difference means nothing as one gets older, but in high school, it seems like a big difference. I always loved younger women. I am getting ahead of myself here, but I have always subscribed to a memorable quote often attributed to Tony Curtis (a.k.a. Bernard Schwartz—true): "I could never date anyone old enough to be my wife." Yes, it's a memorable and funny quote, but not one to live your life by, as you shall see in subsequent chapters. Although, as I understand it, it has generally worked for Tony—lucky guy.

Roslyn was a dark-haired, dark-eyed kewpie doll with

a great figure. She was cute as a dewdrop, and she knew it. These looks were, of course, post-braces and nose job—a seeming prerequisite for Jewish teenage girls. She was from one of those families with many daughters, each one more beautiful than the other. How does that happen? It must be something in the water—in this case, in Cleveland's water supply, as she, too, was originally from Cleveland.

Roslyn and I dated my entire senior year. You would think that I would remember more about our relationship, but frankly, I don't. What I do remember most of all was our breakup at the end of my senior year—heartache.

On or about my eighteenth birthday, lovely Roslyn broke up with me, and I was devastated. I was completely heartbroken for the first but, regrettably, not the last time in my life. You know the feeling—like a truck has driven across your chest. Horrible! Of course, you fantasize about all the good things about her, even if they weren't true. You don't know how you will ever get over it. You call her on the phone just to hear her voice and hang up. You even peer over her fence to see if she is with anyone else.

Of course, today this kind of behavior might be considered "stalking" by some, and can have rather unfortunate consequences. And, once, as I was peering over her fence one night with my friend David (you met him earlier at my bar mitzvah), I was stopped by a policeman and told by him to forget about her and go home. A policeman dispensing advice to the lovelorn. I think his badge actually said "Officer Dr. Phil." That's something you're not going to see on the next episode of *Cops*.

Anyway, one does finally get over such things. Time heals all wounds, or as Groucho would say, "time wounds all heels." I wish it were so.

One funny story that I later heard about her concerned her engagement to her future husband. Okay, I know that hearsay is not admissible in court, but it is a great story, and having known her and her family, it was undoubtedly true. After she was presented with an engagement ring by her future husband, her parents had him return the ring and exchange it, as the diamond had not been large enough to satisfy them. Her fiancée dutifully bought her a larger ring. Cute, huh? I would like to think that I would have reacted a bit differently, and I thank God that I didn't marry into that family.

Twenty years later, I ran into her again. She had been married for almost twenty years, had two children, and was about to get divorced. Another ring dispute? She had just had her breasts lifted ("Not enlarged, just lifted," she emphasized to me), and she was quite proud of them. Yes, they felt fine. We didn't have much more to talk about other than her breasts, and I quickly realized that she might be even more shallow than I was, if such a thing was possible. Obviously, there was no "click" remaining, and we went our separate ways. I do wish her and her breasts nothing but the best. And I mean it.

Conclusion: When it's over, it's over. Let it go. I know it is tough—maybe one of the toughest things that you will ever do—but some things are just not meant to be. If these sound like overused clichés, they are, but you will find that they are all true and can all be applied to life, love, and the pursuit of happiness.

Chapter Six: The College Boy

Sophomore to Senior Year: Stacey the Model

We called her "the model," we being the guys who used to take the bus daily from our dorm to campus at the University of Colorado. We called her the model as she was tall and statuesque and carried herself in an elegant manner. Stacey had long, brown hair down to her lovely hips, beautiful hazel eyes, a cute turned-up nose, and a glorious smile. Picture Katherine Ross in *The Graduate* ("Elaine! Elaine!"). And each and every one of us was afraid to approach her.

However, one night toward the end of my sophomore year, we ran into each other at a bus stop, and the rest is history, which is to say that we began a romantic relationship. College was out for the summer, though. I was stuck in Dallas, she was in Denver, and the days could not pass quickly enough for either of us. This was true love—at least I thought so, and still do.

Finally I got back to school for my junior year, and Stacey and I made love for the first time—and, I mean the first time for both of us. It was kinda romantic when looking back on it, at least until she started to bleed shortly after we completed our love-making.

Thinking myself a man of the world, I applied a cold

compress to the affected area, but the bleeding would not stop. Finally we went to the University clinic. I was not allowed in with her, but she told me later that they had to stitch her up. Horror. "They," whoever "they" were, also told her that we had "done it wrong." To this day, I am still confused. How can two people do it wrong? Anyway, we continued doing it, and apparently started doing it right, as we had a very satisfactory sex life during our three years together.

Specifically, I remember one hot day during summer school. Stacey was wearing white short-shorts, we were both twenty-one years old, and we made love five times in about an hour and a half (a record I now approach only in my dreams). We were very compatible and good friends. Maybe I was learning a lesson or two. I even took her home to Dallas to meet my parents. She and my mom disliked each other instantly. To this day, I don't know what the problem was, but at the time it posed a problem for me, because I wanted my mom and girlfriend to get along. Today I'm not so sure that I would care quite as much.

I asked my mom about this episode in preparation for this book. She said that she and Stacey had driven past our temple, and my mom had pointed it out to Stacey as the place where my sister had recently gotten married. My mom felt that Stacey, as a Catholic, was probably offended for some reason. I just felt like a precursor to Rodney King in thinking, "Can't we all just get along?" Unfortunately we all just couldn't get along.

In any event, we graduated and I returned to Dallas for law school, without Stacey. Why? It was not a wise move in retrospect. She had been the only girl that I had known in the biblical sense, and I felt, rightly or wrongly, that I needed to meet and sleep with more girls before getting married.

Our, by now, long-distance relationship limped along for almost a year, until inevitably, she found someone else. It served me right, but I was devastated (shades of Roslyn ... remember her?). It took me quite a while to get over her, but I think I finally made it. However, for the sake of curiosity, I did recently hire a private detective to track her down. He did—in Oakland, California. He gave her my particulars and told her that I would like to hear from her. I am still waiting. Don't worry, I am not holding my breath.

Finally, the following fact is one that is important for all guys to recognize. Remember this: all girls turn into their mothers, sooner or later. By this I mean that all girls will start looking, if not acting, like their mothers over time. As I mentioned, Stacey was a Katherine Ross, circa 1968. Unfortunately, her mother was an Eleanor Roosevelt, circa 1945. The last time I saw Stacey—fully ten years after our relationship ended—I could see Eleanor start to make great inroads into Katherine. Things probably did work out for the best after all, or did they?

It is interesting to note that I became well known as the guy who was dating Stacey. I am sure that my male classmates would look at us and wonder, "What the hell does she see in him?" During my undergraduate years and thereafter, I was known as the lucky guy in the business school who dated the girl with the long, brown hair. Even years later, after I became an attorney, those people who attended the business school with me didn't necessarily remember me, but did remember that there was someone who was always hanging out with Stacey, and when I told them it was me, they seemed to put the pieces into place and remember me for the simple fact that I was Stacey's boyfriend. I guess it is just nice being remembered for any reason, even if it is for something having very little to do with you.

Conclusion: Well, she was my best friend for a very important three years of my life, so in retrospect, and despite her mother/Eleanor, I may have made a mistake in not marrying her. But, as another wise old man once told me, the past is the past and never kick yourself over mistakes you may have made in the past. (I'm going to have to stop talking to wise old men.)

Law School: Rhonda, My Very Own Laura Bush

Every couple should have a good "first meeting" story. This one is not my best (see Alina: The Second Ballet Dancer in the next chapter), but it is a pretty good one.

I was clerking after my first year of law school at a law firm in downtown Dallas. Still licking my wounds from the breakup with Stacey, I was anxious to meet someone new. An associate in the firm had told me about a cute and single court reporter who had been in the office taking a deposition just two weeks before I started working there.

I called her and reminded her that we had met at our law office during the deposition (a lie on my part; utter confusion on hers). I asked her if she would like to get together for dinner. She accepted, and we met that night. Smooth—dishonest, but smooth.

She was a sweet, homespun type of girl from Pecos, Texas, with a wonderful personality and a great Texas twang to her voice. The folks loved her. In fact, looking back over all the women in my life, she would have probably made the best wife and mother.

So what was wrong with me? Well, I was still quite shallow at the time. Her figure was a bit fuller than was my wont. In addition, she was a virgin when we met, and the sex was just so-so. I was never very interested in teaching. Although we spent two years together, the relationship did not flourish. This was my fault. I should have been more compassionate in and out of bed. She was quite willing. I was just rather removed from it all. Maybe I was still thinking of Stacey. More likely, I was just thinking of myself.

Later, however, after I moved back to Colorado, she introduced me to the joys of phone sex. How seemingly out-of-character for her and what a turn-on. Here was this sweet, virginal girl from the Bible Belt in Texas telling me all sorts of delightful things over the phone. It was a brand new experience for me, and one that I will always remember.

Whatever happened to Rhonda? She is one of the girls who I did track down recently. She has been happily married for twenty-plus years with two children. And although she has lost her Texas twang, she told me that many people do indeed tell her that she reminds them of Laura Bush. George W. and I could have done much worse.

Conclusion: For all practical purposes, Rhonda was just about perfect. Ultimately, I think that I just did not love her enough to marry her. You can't force it, and you can't fake it (love, that is). At least one of us is extremely happy and content—and I think it is her.

Chapter Seven: The Man

(And I use that term very loosely)
Gayle: The Nonstop Talker

Here I was, finally out of college and law school and actually earning a decent living, but since first grade, I had always been thrown together with girls in my various classes. In most years, finding a girlfriend was like shooting fish in a barrel. (At least I think that the term is "fish" in a barrel. But, why one would want to shoot fish in a barrel or shoot fish at all is beyond me.) In any event, now I was out in the real world. No more would there be first-, second-, or third-day-of-class girls. For that matter, no more would there be any-day-of-class girls. I was now completely on my own. Kinda scary, as I thought about it.

In any event, a fellow co-worker fixed me up with Gayle, a cute, blonde-haired, blue-eyed Jewish girl (yes, you read correctly) from Long Island, New York, who sounded every bit like a Jewish girl from Long Island, New York, for good or ill.

She was a sweet girl and meant well, but she never (and I do mean *never*) stopped talking. As Groucho would say, it was like she was "vaccinated with a phonograph needle." I liked her well enough to bring her to Dallas to meet the folks, and they liked her right away. Still smarting from her experience with Stacey, my mom was on her best behavior to say nothing but nice things, but she pulled me aside after a few days and said, "Doesn't she ever stop talking?" Sheepishly, I had to admit that, no, she did not. Needless to say, it was not a long-lasting relationship.

Conclusion: Nothing profound. She was a sweetheart in many ways, but I am a very quiet person by nature, and she was a nonstop talker. Never the twain shall meet. A relationship is a two-way street with two-way communication—an impossibility if one of the parties never, ever stops talking.

Jodi: The Live-in Lover

When I met her at a party, my first thought was that she was hot. My second thought was that she was an outrageous flirt. My third thought was that she truly did not like or respect men—at least that was the appearance she gave vis-à-vis the men that I saw her flirting with at the party.

That third thought came back to bite me on the ass, and unfortunately, that first thought was what led me to date her for two years—two very long years. However, in the end, my third thought, thank God, actually did save me from marrying her.

She could be charming. As the saying goes, she was great for casuals. My parents met her and liked her, but she could never be a true friend or partner. Beware of any significant other who either puts you down in public, makes you the butt of her jokes, or both. Jodi did both. The very first time it happens, run away and run away fast.

In addition, I was very fortunate to meet her parents.

Her mom was a real ball-buster (just like her), and her dad was a mild-mannered attorney (just like me). Hmm … I just knew that, in twenty years time, these two people would be us. It was very enlightening and very lucky for me that I was able to see it for myself, up close and personal.

Even after almost two years, with the relationship on its last legs, I thought we'd give it another chance by moving in together. This was a big mistake, which led me to the following lessons learned.

Conclusion: Generally, a woman will turn into her mother, for good or ill. As I discussed with regard to Stacey, she will begin to look like her mother. As with Jodi, she will also begin acting like her mother. If you can't stand her mother, watch out. In addition, if her mother treats her father like crap, expect the same from her. And never move in together in the hopes that it will salvage a tottering relationship. It will never work. Finally, once you realize a relationship is not working out, end it immediately. Don't stay in it an extra day longer, and certainly not months or years longer. Life is too short. Don't waste time.

Just one more thing … Jodi was the first girl, to the best of my knowledge, who was not faithful to me. Winston Churchill once said that a man loves his friend because he or she stands by him at doubtful moments. It is obvious that Jodi never read Churchill, for she was certainly not one to stand by her man. As I recall, I had just been operated on to correct a deviated septum. Jodi drove me back from the hospital, tucked me into bed to recover on my own, and went skiing for the weekend with "a friend." Such disregard and disrespect. It was very sad, really. So, as a result, I started an affair with …

Melissa: The First Ballet Dancer

Melissa had been a principal dancer with a local ballet company before injury put a halt to her career. She was cute in a Molly Ringwald (remember her?) sort of way, and I fell for her. She was from a very wealthy family. Her father, a prominent local attorney, hated my guts. Then again, I didn't feel too bad about it, as he had never even met me. I guess he just didn't like the idea of an older guy dating his cherished younger, virginal (yeah, right!) daughter. To paraphrase Groucho in *Duck Soup*, "He was protecting her honor, which was more than she ever did."

Speaking of Molly Ringwald, I was a big fan of hers way back during her heyday. When she made the cover of *Time* magazine, I wrote to the editor of *Time* asking if she could be on the cover every week. I thought that request was very clever as apparently did the editor, and my letter was published. But I never did hear from Molly, and she never made the cover of *Time* again. A coincidence? I'm not so sure.

Anyway, back to Melissa ... Unfortunately, she had all the problems one would associate with a ballet dancer: self-absorption, selfishness, anorexia, bulimia, and assorted other problematic behaviors. By the way, avoid all women who actually have a professional doctor's scale in their bathroom—a bad sign. (What can I say? I was getting back at Jodi.) Melissa also shared Jodi's attitude about being faithful. The thing that stands out for me the most is a phrase that I heard often in Groucho's writings about Chico, which applied exactly to Melissa: she never failed to disappoint me in the fact that she would disappoint me. Did you follow that? If not, read that sentence again. I dodged another bullet, didn't I?

People (actually, just men) have often asked me what it is like to sleep with a ballet dancer. Well, all ballet dancers are different as all attorneys are different. It reminds me of a Seinfeld episode where Jerry is dating a Romanian gymnast. He wants to break up with her before sleeping with her, as he just doesn't like her all that much. But Kramer talks him into it, as he wants to live vicariously through the delights that he believes Jerry is about to experience. After the deed is done, Kramer gallops into Jerry's apartment to get all the juicy (sorry!) details. Jerry's response is that "it was all just so ordinary." That has been my experience as well.

Conclusion: Well, I guess that I said it all: self-absorption, selfishness, anorexia, etc. What was I thinking? One important lesson relearned was that you just can't help some people. Even if I was well-equipped to help her with her issues, I am not at all sure that I could have succeeded. But I was not so equipped, and the end result would always be that she would drag me down to her level. Ultimately, surround yourself with mentally and spiritually healthy people, and you will be better off.

Sachi: From France Nuyen to Yoko Ono

Yet another bullet dodged ... but I am getting ahead of myself. People who know Sachi now would never believe it, but when I first met her she was beautiful in a France Nuyen sort of way. (Does anyone remember her? The movie *South Pacific*? Anyone? Oh well, another Google search is in order.) Long, dark hair, beautiful complexion, great figure, extremely bright (a CPA), and a lot of fun. Also, she was two years older than me. It was quite novel for me. I met her at an art auction where she was prancing around and displaying the artwork and herself. She was quite charming, actually, but ... that was then.

My downfall was in meeting her eighteen-month-old daughter, Jennifer. Did you ever meet a child and fall instantly in love? I did so with Jennifer. Hell, I even changed diapers. I must say that, to this day, some of the best times of my life were spent playing with that beautiful child. I know you are way ahead of me here, but I continued the relationship with Sachi for far too long, so that I would not lose the relationship with Jennifer.

As I said, when I first met Sachi, she seemed delightful, but over time, she just became mean (or maybe she was always bitter, and I was just slow in realizing it). She came from a very strict household, and there did not appear to be a lot of affection between parents and siblings or between siblings. I noticed that right away and was bothered by it. Sachi's own household was very similar in all its negative aspects. She had a very troubled relationship with her older daughter, although a much better relationship with Jennifer. Finally, she shared with Jodi the trait of putting me down in public or making me the butt of her jokes. As she became older and more bitter, France Nuyen morphed into Yoko Ono. (What was John thinking?)

Oh, well, at least I obtained personal financial advice, free of charge. For example, Sachi twisted my arm to open up an IRA—sound financial advice. However, I would have gladly paid a professional for that advice in return for a number of years of my life back.

I made another terrible mistake. One of my oldest

corporate clients was looking for a chief financial officer. I felt that Sachi fit the bill, so I introduced them, and she was hired. One year later, she was fired for various and sundry reasons. She sued. Two years and many thousands of dollars in attorney's fees later (I had recused myself), she lost the case. Justice was done, but I felt like I had been in a whirlpool of hate, lies, and deceit the entire time. Now, if a client is looking for an employee, I urge them to check out Monster.com.

Conclusion: More wasted years. Please dear readers, never, ever stay in a relationship longer than good sense dictates. And never, ever stay in a relationship because of your fondness for the kinder. It does you no good, it does the mother no good, and it certainly does the child no good. It might be painful. It will be painful. But move on with your life. And finally, never mix business with pleasure. Keep your girlfriend(s) and your clients separate for all purposes. Never try to play "matchmaker" in that regard. You may end up losing both.

Michelle: The Rich Taiwanese Virgin

I had heard from a co-worker that there was a young, attractive Asian woman (this was during my Asian phase) who worked in a local restaurant. Naturally, I went to check her out. We met, seemed to click, and began dating. I was still smooth back then.

Michelle was at least fifteen years younger than me and a virgin. She was from a fabulously wealthy family (her father owned many restaurants, including the one where we met) and lived with her parents and sisters in a palatial mansion. The inside of the house was filled with Chinese antiques and reminded me of one of the Imperial Palaces in the Forbidden City in Beijing. Yes, I have been there.

I should have treated her home as a forbidden city myself, as her father seemed to have nothing but disdain for me. I never even met the man (shades of Melissa here?). I clearly remember walking up her driveway to introduce myself and shake his hand, and he did an about-face and headed back into the house. Talk about rejection.

Anyway, Michelle was crafty and seemed to like me, but most of all, she wanted to lose her virginity, so she set up a situation whereby she seduced me in her bedroom. It was all very professionally done, and in looking back on it, I give her great credit for her planning. As I said, she was a virgin, and as I alluded to in talking about Rhonda, only bed a virgin if you are truly in love with her and are willing to spend a great deal of time teaching her all the intricacies in matters sexual.

I enjoy teaching my clients about the law. I do not necessarily enjoy the other kind of teaching—personal preference. Everyone is different. However, I do not envy the Muslim terrorists who will find themselves with seventy virgins (or is it seventy-two virgins?) on their hands in paradise. That sounds a bit more like hell than paradise to me. That's just one Jew's opinion. *Shalom.*

Conclusion: Well, I have wracked my brain, but cannot come up with any conclusions regarding my relationship with Michelle, so I will just wish her well and move on.

Marcy: The Artistic Street Urchin

Wow. Every guy should have a Marcy in his life at least one time or another, or maybe not.

One day, I was eating at a Burger King (something I try not to do too often), and out of the corner of my eye, I saw a girl in another booth. She was a sweet, doe-eyed brunette, and was very cute. She appeared to be filling out a job application, which told me she was at least sixteen years old (perhaps a faulty assumption). From her looks, she could have been twelve or twenty-four. It was hard to tell. As it turned out, she was eighteen years old. I was much older.

She completed her application and left. But to where? I made it my mission to try to find her and speak to her. This incident occurred in a strip mall, and I finally located her in a Hallmark store. I talked with her. We exchanged pleasantries and seemed to hit it off right away. She told me that she was hungry, so we went back to my place. I made her a peanut butter and jelly sandwich, and we ended up in bed. (Apparently, I make a *mean* peanut butter and jelly sandwich.) I distinctly remember her asking me to tell her that I loved her, which I declined to do. My heart did go out to her. She seemed like a lost soul, and I was determined to help her out—mixed motives on my part.

Her story was basically as follows: she was from an affluent family from Philadelphia who had basically disowned her. She had just enough money to have an unfurnished apartment and pay for tuition at a local art school. Marcy was actually a brilliant artist. As for other necessities, like food, clothing, and art supplies, she had to beg, borrow, and steal (mostly steal). She was very street smart and was quite proud of the fact that she was able to pass for twelve years old so as to enable her to buy a child's bus pass.

Marcy was also very experienced in all matters sexual,

and that was a big turn-on. She related to me that she had lost her virginity to another woman (!) at the age of twelve. I don't know if that was true, but she certainly did seem to know her way around the bedroom. She also liked to play games (Daddy and Little Girl, etc.). Quite frankly, I thought she was fascinating on a number of levels. But there was also a certain disconnect, as I was used to dating girls who could actually afford their own groceries and were not reduced to stealing.

A perfect example of how differently we thought about things is illustrated by the following story: I dropped by her apartment unannounced one night. Apparently, she was "entertaining" another boyfriend of hers named Lincoln (not "Abraham," I presume). Marcy was looking at me through the door's peephole and saw me reach into my back pocket. Immediately, she opened the door, fearing that I was reaching for a gun. A gun? Not only did I not own a gun, I wouldn't even know how to use one. I was actually reaching for my wallet to write her a note on one of my business cards. Talk about viewing the world from a different point of view.

I also must admit that I kept Marcy to myself. I did not bring her when socializing with friends. I did not take her to any law firm functions, nor did I take her to places where I might run into other friends or co-workers. Could I have been ashamed of her? Possibly. I also would not allow her to be at my townhome in my absence. I could just picture returning to an empty house. Could I have not trusted her? Definitely.

It was not fated to last, but the relationship limped along fitfully for almost nine months, although it was not exclusive, on either part, by any means. Then, just as suddenly as she appeared, she disappeared. That was probably a good thing. It was a fascinating experience, but one which I would not care to repeat. God bless her. I hope life has been kind to her since our brief encounter. I heard through the grapevine that she is now married with three children. Good for her. I also heard that she became a devout Quaker, honestly. No disrespect to Quakers, but I find that fact somewhat amusing.

Speaking of parents ... okay, I wasn't speaking of parents, but I will now. My late father was, and my mother still is, wonderful (part of "The Greatest Generation"). They retired to Sarasota, Florida, after their children moved away from Dallas. Don't all parents live in Florida? I think that it is a federal law. (As for my parents, think Mr. and Mrs. Seinfeld ... don't think Mr. and Mrs. Costanza.) On occasion, I would envision my "girlfriend *du jour*" meeting the parents. I imagine getting off the plane with her, walking past the giant statue of DeSoto at the Sarasota airport, and taking the escalator down to the baggage claim where one of my parents would be waiting for us (the other would be standing by the car in the no-parking zone). I would get one of two reactions to my girlfriend. The first would be a sincere smile and a showing of happiness and approval. The second would be a smile through gritted teeth saying to her "nice to meet you," and then in a private moment, I would get a dope-slap and the question, "What are you thinking? Is this how we raised you?" These reactions would apply to both mom and dad equally. Unfortunately, Marcy would have engendered reaction number two: "the dope slap reaction." No question about it. 'Nuff said.

Conclusion: Very simple. If you care at all about what

your parents think (and you should, to some extent), avoid those girls who would engender the dope-slap reaction. It's better for you, it's better for the girl, and it's better for your parents. Even if you don't care what your parents think, it is still a good barometer to use in determining whether or not you should enter into or stay in a relationship.

Li (meaning "beautiful"): The Chinese Princess

I met Li in a restaurant where she, like Michelle, was working as a waitress. I have tried to hit on numerous hostesses and waitresses in the past. There are some restaurants where I still can't show my face. Thank God there is a high turnover in these positions so that I am generally not banned for life. Anyway, unbeknown to me, Li was not a poor immigrant waitress from China. She was going to the University of Denver and was working part-time to alleviate boredom. She certainly did not need to work.

Indeed, she was not only one of the most beautiful women I had ever met, but she was from a very privileged background in China. Her father was a retired general in the Communist Chinese Army, and she grew up in Beijing with servants, nannies, a driver, and so on. So much for communism in the People's Republic of China. I often wondered what meeting the general would have been like. Would he have liked me or would he have tried to cut my head off with his sword? Alas, I never got the opportunity to find out.

Li was also a successful businesswoman and a model, both in Denver and in China. In fact, she was my first and only calendar girl. She appeared on a calendar (fully clothed) in China. I thought that was so cool!

And, yes, I was in love with her, and for some reason, Li was also in love with me. There were certainly cultural differences and communication difficulties, but she was so sweet and kind that I did not feel that these posed insurmountable obstacles. We dated on and off for a number of years. All that time, I pondered marriage with her. Sometimes, you can overanalyze matters. Just do it, as the Nike ads tell us. Finally I summoned up the courage, bought an engagement ring, and was prepared to ask her to marry me.

I had it all planned out in my mind. (That was one of my mistakes.) I would get on one knee, give her the ring, and propose. Of course she would hug me with tears in her eyes and say, "Yes, yes, of course, I will marry you!" That was the script in my mind anyway. The reality was that she looked at me, put the ring on, and said, "I'll think about it." I was crushed. Later, by the time she was truly ready to accept, I had already met someone else.

Timing is everything in life. I don't know who first said that, but I won't be the last one to say it, nor will it be the last time that I will say it. Did you follow that?

Of course, she kept the ring. Isn't it the law that the ring has to be returned if the marriage does not occur? At least that's what Judge Judy says. I get all my legal expertise from Judge Judy—don't tell my clients. I'll have to research that issue more carefully. (Speaking of Judge Judy, this brief story will tell you the lengths that I have gone to with respect to meeting women. I was watching Judge Judy one evening and saw the most beautiful girl as a defendant on the show. I was so entranced by her that I wrote to the show's producers to see if I could get some information about her. Alas, there was no reply. Nothing ventured, nothing gained.)

In any event, Li and I have kept in touch over the years, but things could never be the same, especially now that she has permanently relocated to China. I still blame her for not saying yes. There are certain things that are out of our control. Maybe if I had been more persistent? Who knows? Speculation is useless at this point in time.

Conclusion: Again, don't waste precious time (a recurring theme here). Ask her to marry you sooner rather than later. If she says "yes," great. If she says "no," lick your wounds and move on. And always try to get the ring back—you can always find a willing buyer on eBay.

Alina: The Second Ballet Dancer

Like I said, every relationship should have a good first meeting story. This story is my best, so far. I think you'll like it, too.

I was still dating Li, on and off, and we had stopped at a Blockbuster Video around 8:30 p.m. on a Saturday evening to rent a video. I was walking around the store, and suddenly I was mesmerized. Before me stood an Audrey Hepburn look-alike, circa 1952 (*Roman Holiday*). She was holding the video, *The American President*, starring Michael Douglas—the movie that Li wanted to see. But there was only one copy. This girl tells me that we can have the video, as she had already seen the movie, and then she leaves.

I was beside myself. I didn't get a name, a type of car, or anything. Needless to say, I could not concentrate on Michael Douglas that evening. For the next three consecutive Saturdays, I showed up at Blockbuster Video at exactly 8:30 p.m. to see if I could find her. Nothing.

Slowly but surely, I forgot about her ... but not really. A few weeks went by, and I was jogging by my townhome complex one day, when across the street was this same girl walking a couple of dogs. I immediately went up to her and reminded her of our video-store encounter. She did not recall. I introduced myself, and she told me her name, Alina. I gave her my business card and told her to call me if she ever wanted to get together for sushi. (I thought the offer of sushi would sound sophisticated.)

As it turned out, she was house- and dog-sitting for a neighbor of mine. I was obsessed. I had to think of something cute to do to get her attention, so I bought the movie *Funny Face* (starring a very young Audrey Hepburn and a very old Fred Astaire) and left it at my neighbor's door with a card and photo asking her to call me. Nothing.

Months went by, and I didn't see her again until the next summer. I was shopping at my local Safeway, and she passed by. At least I thought it was her. Younger girls can change a lot from year to year, and I had no idea how old she was (twenty years old as it turned out). I told myself that I would pick up one more grocery item and then would go talk with her. But by the time I did so, she was gone. I searched the Safeway aisles for an hour. Again, nothing.

A week later, I was sweeping out my garage, and she drove by. Coincidence? Karma? Kismet? Stalking? I didn't know, but I did take down her license plate number, went to the Colorado DMV office, and got her name and address. (Please note, you can no longer do that in the State of Colorado under what, I believe, they call "The Barry Law.")

Well, I wrote to her again, enclosing a photo. She did call, we went out that same evening, and we dated for the next four years. I wish that I could say it was four years of bliss.

There were danger signs. Alina was a ballet dancer and, unfortunately, somewhat self-absorbed. My first clue came upon entering her apartment. She had photos of herself everywhere I looked. Later, there were more danger signs. She had lied to her mother that she was still attending college, and so was receiving tuition money from mom, but was spending it on ballet lessons and other assorted living expenses. Another danger sign came when I asked her if she ever wanted children, and she said "No, because I never want anyone to treat me the way that I treat my mother."

Finally, I never felt totally secure in the relationship. I always felt that if, God forbid, I should get sick, lose my job, etc., she would be gone. I felt that very strongly, and nothing that she ever did caused me to change my mind or rethink that potential problem. This is not a good sign for a healthy, long-term relationship, but I was in love with her, so I noted but chose to ignore all of these signs and potential problems. As they say, love is blind. And as Dandy Don Meredith once said, "they" is a very reliable source.

Alina was wonderful in a hundred different ways, and we had many interests in common, such as ballet, theater, opera, classical music, movies, fine food, and the like. But over time, our relationship developed into a quasi-platonic relationship. I still loved her and, don't tell anyone, probably still do to this day. However, I think that I also started taking her and the relationship for granted. This was a big mistake in many ways.

As I said, after four bittersweet years, it was over. Alina had just been accepted to attend the Kirov Ballet Academy of Washington, D.C., which is a great honor. (Okay, so we fudged her age a bit on the application—sue me.) Of course she could not afford the tuition, so I, the altruistic and by now ex-boyfriend, Barry, paid her tuition for a year hoping that, at the end of the year, she could audition for ballet companies from all over the world. Unfortunately, she injured herself during the audition period, and her ballet career was over. In retrospect, I think that I may have wanted a ballet career for Alina more than she wanted it for herself. We never saw each other again. In fact, she never even thanked me. No good deed goes unpunished. I am afraid that that statement is as true today as it was when first uttered all those many years ago.

The good, nay, great news ... I got custody of our perfect black Cocker Spaniel puppy, Zorro, who was the light of my life until his untimely passing. So very sad.

Conclusion: No girl is perfect. No relationship is perfect. And, in this case, there were certainly danger signs and potential pitfalls. But, if the girl/relationship is important enough to you, never, ever take either for granted. Keep conscious of not doing so every day. If you love her, let her know it, in ways large and small, every single day. I know it sounds easy, but it is actually quite difficult. But do try—you will thank me. I just wish that I had done so. Where were you, dear reader, when I needed your advice?

Afterthought: In reading and rereading this section on "The Little One," as I called her, it occurred to me that relationships are full of contradictions. On the one hand, I loved her with all my heart; on the other hand, I was fairly certain that we could not build a life together. In retrospect, I should have gone with what my heart told me and worked hard at making the relationship a success.

Barry: Licking My Wounds

And then, I took a break from dating. As much of a chore as it has been for you to read of these relationships, it has been an even greater chore for me to live them, so I took a year off and spent quality time with Zorro. In retrospect, I am so glad that I did so. And then I met …

Emily: The Exotic Dancer

I was in the habit of frequenting a sushi restaurant near my home, and I became friendly with the manager. The manager was a very creative marketer for the restaurant. For example, she had asked all single patrons for their photos and decreed that every Wednesday night would be singles night. I was not really interested in participating in singles night, but I did give her a photo. Later, she showed me a photo of a very attractive blonde who wanted to meet me. I took her name and number and called her.

As it turns out, her name was Emily, and she was, by her own description, an "exotic dancer." Where I grew up, we would have called her a "stripper." She had aspirations for a music career and likened herself to Gwen Stefani— no way. There was nothing terribly interesting or exciting about Emily, I promise. Suffice it to say, she was very sexy, but a bit coarse and uneducated. I wasn't seeing anyone else at the time, so I continued to see Emily.

One date particularly stands out in my mind. Emily had me take her to a store specializing in "adult" products and wanted me to buy dog collars for the both of us. Idiot that I was, I meekly complied. They were both black, felt collars surrounded by rhinestones. I never asked her what they were for—frankly, I did not want to know. In any event, we never did anything with the collars, and the relationship ended shortly thereafter. But I had a perfect use for mine: Zorro looked so handsome in his new collar.

Our last date was also somewhat memorable. I had been invited by friends, the owners and operators of a local ballet academy, to a charity benefit for their ballet school. As the only person I was seeing at the time was Emily, I brought her with me, hoping against hope that she would not do or say anything to humiliate me. While she didn't quite fit in (to put it mildly), I survived the evening with my dignity intact.

As an aside, I do recall that she wore a very short skirt to the event. I remember that the men (mostly husbands) at the event kept looking at her with lust in their eyes, while the women (mostly wives) in the room stared daggers at her. It was a very interesting dynamic.

Having run the course of the relationship, we stopped seeing each other. I am sure that neither of us grieved about the end of our relationship.

Conclusion: Simple. As with a number of women you have met in this book, I was loathe to introduce Emily to family, friends, or co-workers. Avoid all such women who might become an embarrassment. You will know who they are instinctively. Follow your instincts.

Olga: The Last, and Certainly Least, Ballet Dancer

As it turns out, my friends at the ballet academy were none too impressed with Emily and decided they would fix me up with one of their dancers named Olga, a cute Siberian girl. What they should have realized was that Olga was not a big (or even small) improvement over Emily. God bless them. I am sure they meant well, but Olga was a walking (or dancing) disaster.

As I said, Olga was a cute girl. She was a wisp of a girl with blonde hair, blue eyes, and a ballet dancer's body. But she was in this country illegally and cleaned houses to make ends meet. As all of her money was made under the table, she paid no taxes. Whatever money she did earn, she gambled away on trips to Las Vegas. In addition, Olga spoke English very poorly, was not at all interested in improving her language skills, and had a dour Siberian personality. If that wasn't quite enough to put a man off, she had gray teeth. (A doctor friend of mine told me that, in the former countries of the Soviet Union, they used to treat children with tetracycline, which would turn their teeth gray from the inside, so teeth-whitening would not be an option.) While my heart goes out to Olga and those like her, I must admit that when I was not in her company, I affectionately referred to her as "Gray Tooth." (Kind of like "Braveheart"—okay, maybe not like it at all.) People have asked me, "Did you kiss her?" I have sheepishly admitted that, "Yes, I did." I know, I know.

Frankly, even a few years ago, I would not have given

her the time of day, but one gets lonely, desperate, and (you fill in the blank) at times. I set out to warm her cold Siberian heart, but it was not meant to be. It was a relationship in name only. Against my better judgment, I tried to make it work. She did absolutely nothing to further the relationship. Our last night together was on a Christmas Day evening. I gave her wonderful presents, which were not reciprocated. She cooked me an inedible Russian meal. We agreed to not see each other again, and "Merry Christmas," we never did see each other again.

A few months later, she had remarried (her second marriage), and within six months was divorced again. Two marriages and divorces before the age of thirty—a future Siberian Elizabeth Taylor (with gray teeth) in the making.

The near-relationship with Olga reminds me of what can result from desperation and lowering one's standards. Have you ever driven home after a night of clubbing, and having failed to meet anyone, started looking into the windows of cars next to you for that one last possible pick-up? To me, that was Olga, but it could also apply to any other number of girls who I may have met and spent a brief amount of time with over the years. And yes, Olga would definitely have generated the dope-slap reaction from my parents, as discussed above with respect to Marcy.

Conclusion: Whatever you do, don't ever lower your standards just to be with someone. It is much better to be alone. I was lucky. I lowered my standards to be with Olga for a mere six months or so. It was misguided and stupid, but I have known others who have lowered their standards for a lifetime of misery. Be smart. To the Olgas of the world, just say "Nyet!"

Kelly: The Felon

Okay, okay, she wasn't really a felon, but she was too close for my comfort—much too close.

When I first met her, she seemed intelligent (notice how I started off with that one?) and charming, with a very nice figure. I even took her to my law firm's Christmas party that year, and she seemed to fit in just fine, with no embarrassments.

She specifically told me (or at least, led me to believe) that she was gainfully employed at a bank, that she had never been married, and that she had no children. The subject of a criminal record never came up in our initial conversations. (Should it be mandatory?)

But every single time that I got together with her, her story would change. She actually did not work at a bank, but had only started an apprentice-type program. Later, she was no longer working at the bank as an apprentice, as the bank had discovered her criminal record. (Yikes. What criminal record?) Her first story was that an ex-boyfriend had failed to pay a cab driver, and she had been charged with theft. Well, that didn't sound quite right. Her next story was that it had to do with some type of domestic-relations offense. I didn't want to know any more and figured that I would never get at the complete truth anyway.

Still later, I learned that she had been married and had a teenage son that her mother had raised from infancy. The truth? You tell me. In any event, it really didn't matter, as there had been too many lies, too much negative information, and all too soon. I decided that I had to stop seeing her, and I did stop. That was the end of Kelly … or so I thought.

A few months later, I got a call from a "girlfriend" of hers asking me to bail her out of jail. The story from her friend was that she had been jailed for a traffic offense. As I was no longer seeing her, I declined the kind invitation. After Kelly got out of jail, she called me. Apparently, her girlfriend was her former cellmate (!), and Kelly explained that she had been unfairly jailed after an altercation at a bar (yet another story). We had dinner one more time—don't ask me why—and I never saw her again. Of course, I am not an avid watcher of the TV show *Cops*, so I may have missed more of her shenanigans.

Conclusion: When one lie rears its ugly head, there are usually more waiting in the wings. Be wary, be diligent, and, if it turns out that she does have a criminal record, don't even think twice about ending it—whether or not you are an attorney.

Chapter Eight: The Good, the Bad, and the Miscellaneous

Brenda: The Hawaiian Affair

After my graduation from college, my father treated my family (my mother, sister and then-brother-in-law, and me) to a week trip in Hawaii. I was anxious to go, but also felt like the proverbial fifth wheel, so I was hoping to meet someone there.

We took a direct flight from Dallas to Honolulu, and I noticed on our flight an adorable girl with short, blonde hair and a pretty face and figure. Apparently she was with a friend and her mother. Yes, I was eavesdropping a bit. I didn't make any moves during the flight, as I just knew that, after the plane landed, we would go our separate ways.

Thank God I was wrong, as we both checked into the Hilton Hawaiian Village Hotel on Waikiki Beach. That first night we met, and it was lust at first sight. Her name was Brenda, and she was from Ida, Louisiana. I was twenty-two, she was seventeen, and not yet being an attorney, I knew nothing about statutory rape or even if it applied in this instance—which I doubt. *Aloha*, Brenda!

I was staying in my parents' room, and even though they got suspicious when my mom found Brenda's slippers under my bed one afternoon, they didn't mind. They liked Brenda, and she became part of our family for the remainder of the trip. What a grand time.

This was the era of sex, drugs, and rock and roll, especially on a Hawaiian trip, and I am afraid Brenda and I indulged in the first two quite extensively. Have you ever had sexual activity on Waikiki Beach at 3:00 a.m.? Well, Waikiki Beach is never deserted at any time of day. I don't know how I had the nerve, but it was that kind of time, and Brenda was that type of companion. The week went by too quickly in a haze of sex, drugs, swimming, touring, eating, and just having the time of my life. As with all good things, it ended all too quickly.

Thankfully, Brenda was on the flight back to Dallas, so we could say our good-byes. We were seated by ourselves in those double seats that are always in the middle of the plane on jumbo jets. We covered our laps with blankets, and she said good-bye in the nicest way she could. At one point, my dad came by to see how we were doing. "Just fine, dad. Please leave." No, Brenda and I didn't quite join the Mile High Club, but we came close. (A bad pun? I'm not so sure.)

Conclusion: No conclusion here, just memories of a very nice girl and very exciting times. I wish you all a Brenda and a romantic trip to Hawaii. But do remember that holiday romances are not real romances. Do not ever confuse the two. I would learn that lesson all too clearly in time (see chapter nine—"Dr. Cathy: Thailand and the Scottish Doctor").

The Hispanic Telemarketer

Have you ever been so lonely or starved for female companionship that you begin flirting with telephone operators or anonymous telemarketers? Well, I did … just once.

As I mentioned, I graduated from the University of Denver College of Law. One evening, I received a call from a girl working as a telemarketer for the DU Alumni Association. I don't remember how it happened, but we seemed to hit it off. One thing led to another, she came over after her shift, and we made love. Yes, it's a bit bizarre, even for me.

I don't remember much about her other than she was Hispanic, she was attractive, and she was my first partner to sport a tattoo. I don't even remember her name, but I do remember her calling me again, and making it clear to her that it was a one-time thing. It was during my immature "love 'em and leave 'em" period, which is amply reflected in this chapter. She was such a nice girl that, in retrospect, I wish I had given her at least half a chance. I guess that I was just too wrapped up in meeting and mating many women.

Conclusion: One-night stands are clearly overrated, if indeed anyone rates them highly at all. I guess they are a part of an active dating life. But may I suggest a good book, movie, or dog walk as much better substitutes? Believe me, spiritually speaking, those substitutes are much healthier.

Elizabeth: The Drinker

Elizabeth—dear, beautiful, troubled Elizabeth. She could have walked into the Playboy headquarters and become an instant centerfold. She was that attractive. Elizabeth was a dark-haired goddess (picture Vivien Leigh in *Gone With the Wind*) with a "form for mortal sin." (I think I got that great line from Katharine Hepburn in the movie *The Lion in Winter*.) Anyway, Elizabeth was almost perfect in every way. To quote Homer, she was a "queen of soft desire." (You didn't think that I could quote Homer, did you?) Unfortunately, she had a problem with alcohol—at least it appeared so to me. She reminds me of the old joke: "Does she drink? Yes, but only to excess." That was Elizabeth.

I met her when she was temping as a receptionist for a law firm that I once worked for. Repeat after me: never date a co-worker. It could be disastrous on a whole number of different levels. More on that a little later.

Our first date was a casual dinner date. I knew something was wrong when she had downed three mixed drinks before we finished our appetizers. Things went downhill from there. Did I learn a lesson? No.

Our second date was to see the movie *Pinocchio*. Before the movie began, she said she had to go to the restroom and never came back. Later, the next day, she told me that she had run into some friends and went out partying with them. Strange, but did I finally learn a lesson? No.

Our third and last date occurred on a very icy and cold New Year's Eve. She was wearing a slinky dress that showed off all of her curves to great advantage, but I was still very wary. I put my foot down and decreed that she was to have only one mixed drink before the dinner portion of our meal.

I knew that I had lost the battle after she had downed her fourth drink before dinner actually arrived. We got through dinner at about 10:00 p.m., and I felt that I needed to get her home ASAP. Have you ever struggled to navigate a drunken woman in three-inch heels over an icy parking lot? I finally got her into the car and was so disoriented by then that I asked her for directions to her home. She told me, but I felt she was in no condition to give me accurate directions, so I flagged down a cop and asked him for directions. He basically repeated her directions and then ... wham ... Elizabeth smacked me right across the face. Apparently, she was furious that I hadn't listened to her directions. I was just stunned. By that time, I just wanted the night to end and to go home.

When we finally arrived at her place, she invited me inside, and against my better judgment, I went in. In minutes, we were making love. A mistake? You bet. In the middle of the act, she reared back her legs and donkey-kicked me across the room. I was again stunned and speechless.

She then put on her nightgown and began brewing a pot of hot coffee. (Thinking it would be a long night?) Whatever she was thinking, I was thinking that I really needed to get the hell out of there before I was drenched with a pot of scalding hot coffee, so I told her that I had to leave.

She looked at me, coyly pulled up her nightie, and asked, "Don't you want more of this?" In my best Woody Allen impersonation, I said, "Well, it looks very nice, but I'm double-parked, and I've got to feed my goldfish, so I really should be getting home." Within the next hour, I was home safe and sound in my own bed, alone. I considered myself very lucky.

I saw Elizabeth one more time. She was tending her garden and told me she was on the wagon. I hope, for her sake, that she stayed there—otherwise, what a waste.

Conclusion: Elizabeth was my first, and last, experience with someone who drank a great deal. And, of course, I was, and am, a lightweight when it comes to alcohol, but if you find yourself involved with a person who drinks a great deal, I wish you the best of luck. My very limited experience is that there is nothing that you can do for the other person unless he or she wants to stop drinking. If he or she doesn't want to stop, you either have to leave or commit yourself to a life sentence of anguish and despair. Good luck.

Sandy: The Receptionist

Have I mentioned that you should never date a co-worker? Have I ever followed my own advice? You be the judge (and jury).

Her name was Sandy, and she was a very sweet girl with light brown hair and a beautiful smile. She was also quite a good receptionist at one of my prior law firms. I believe Sandy had just gotten engaged to be married. We never talked about it, but I think she wanted one last fling before matrimony. Not that I minded, but as I recall, it was not my idea. Not that it matters.

During that very brief affair, we found ourselves alone in the office at 5:00 p.m. one hot afternoon. All of the other attorneys were elsewhere, and all the staff had just gone home. One thing led to another, and we found ourselves on the sixth-floor stairwell enjoying the solitude of the building by making love. I felt fairly secure about not being interrupted, as it was a six-floor building. What I found out later, and what she apparently knew, was that there was a seventh floor where all the janitorial personnel had their offices, so getting caught was a real possibility. I often wondered whether she kept that information from me, knowing that I would never have gone with her if I had known. I guess I'll never know the answer to that question.

Sandy did indeed get married. I went to the wedding. I always feel odd going to a wedding where I have slept with the bride. It is a strange experience on so many levels. In any event, I hope it worked out for her.

Conclusion: Take my advice. Never have sexual relations with anyone in the workplace. It is a bad idea for a number of reasons. Chiefly, a sexual-harassment lawsuit can ruin you professionally and financially—a very good reason indeed for listening to this attorney. Now if I would only listen to my own advice, everything would be fine. But as the saying goes, an attorney who represents himself or herself has a fool for a client.

Lera: The Office Manager and the Chinese Fire Drill

Have I mentioned that … Okay, I guess I have mentioned it. Same law firm, different employee—no wonder this law firm is no longer in existence.

Her name was Lera, and she was a pretty blonde, Southern girl with a charming Southern accent and great legs. She was also having an affair with the senior partner of the firm, who I will call Bob, because that was his name. Lera and I had "been together" only a couple of times. She was the only girl who I've ever been with who actually lit up a cigarette after sex—a big turn-off. Anyway, back to our story.

It was a hot April afternoon, and I just dropped in on Lera after work. It was about 5:45 p.m., and she was getting ready to go to the theater with Bob. He was to pick her up at 6:00 p.m., but Lera wanted a "quickie," so we engaged. During that brief moment of passion, one of my eyes was on Lera; the other was on the clock. I finished at about 5:50 p.m., leaving Lera completely unsatisfied. I had to get the hell out of there, so by 5:55 p.m., I had sneaked out the back stairwell, yelling to Lera behind me that she could come over later if she wanted. I left without Bob seeing me. I felt that I had dodged a bullet and just wanted to go home to the peace and serenity of my house. Little did I know what was in store for me.

I went home and Melissa stopped by (see chapter seven). One thing led to another, and we ended up in bed. All of a sudden (it was about 9:00 p.m.), I heard a pounding on my front door. It was Lera, her hormones raging. At the same time, the phone rang, and it was Jodi (chapter seven, again) calling from out of town. So here I was: Melissa in bed; Lera pounding on the door; and Jodi on the phone. Grand Central Station was never busier. It was like a Marx Brothers movie or a Three Stooges short. (Call me Shemp!) So what did I do? I didn't answer the door. I got off the phone. And I showed Melissa the door. Whew!

I don't relate this story with any amount of pride or satisfaction. In fact, it sort of makes me feel a bit disgusted with myself. I felt the same way at the time. But since I am trying to relate all stories that may be of some interest, this one deserves its place alongside the others. Did I learn anything from this episode? Yes: don't be such a goddamned pig. Maybe I am being too hard on myself, but it certainly wasn't one of my finest hours.

Conclusion: A Chinese fire drill is defined as a state of utter confusion. I tend to be a bit of an anal-compulsive. Utter confusion in any aspect of my life is anathema to me, but utter confusion in one's love life is the worst. If you are like me, avoid it at all costs.

Angelina: The Hair Stylist

She was my new hairstylist. (Now I just get haircuts—they are cheaper. And yes, I still have my hair.) Anyway, she was cute, young, and interested. Do you see a pattern here?

We started dating, but really had nothing in common. In fact, she was a bit common in her interests and attitudes, and she didn't care for sex. She claimed that she had been raped at sixteen years of age and therefore didn't like sex. I was actually quite understanding about it, believe it or not. After a short period of time, I stopped seeing her, as I just didn't feel a great connection.

Fast forward four years ... I was not dating anyone and was starting to think about Angelina. I convinced myself that I had not been very nice to her, I had not given the relationship a chance, and so on. I did some research and located her. She was now styling hair in North (or South?) Carolina. I called her, and we arranged for her to come to Denver to visit me. This was a big mistake. Within the first minute of being with her, I remembered why I had broken up with her in the first place. We had nothing in common. There was no connection. She was, if anything, even more common than when I had known her. The next couple of days seemed like an eternity, but at last she was gone.

Conclusion: Thomas Wolfe once wrote, "You can't go home again." Well, he could just as easily have said, "You can't resurrect an old relationship again." An old relationship is like Humpty Dumpty after the fall. A word to the wise: never try to resuscitate an old relationship. It doesn't work the second time around. With the possible exception of Robert Wagner and Natalie Wood (poor Natalie!), I have never heard of any other.

Jennifer: The Vamp

We literally met as we were passing each other in traffic. That is, for some reason, our eyes locked as she passed me in her car. Of course, I did an immediate U-turn and began my pursuit. She parked her car at a Planned Parenthood facility and went in. I did not follow, but left a note with my business card and placed it on her windshield.

She called. I never asked her about her trip to Planned Parenthood, but we got along well enough on the phone to arrange a meeting. She was young and not particularly well-educated, but she had beautiful blonde hair and exquisite, bright blue eyes—at the time, a good substitute for higher education.

She was a bit of a flirt and a big tease. She used to stare at me with those big, beautiful eyes and say that she was "vamping" me with her eyes. I wish she had vamped me with other parts of her body, but she was resistant to anything other than making out. Frustrating.

She also loved to shop and would always take me with her to Victoria's Secret where she would try on lingerie. Unfortunately, she never left the dressing room or invited me in to see her dressed in that sexy lingerie. Very frustrating.

Ultimately, we had very little in common, and the relationship was going nowhere, so I stopped seeing her. It was only after a couple of years had passed that she got in touch with me again. She had gotten pregnant with someone with whom she was no longer seeing. I didn't ask her what she wanted from me, but just told her that I was busy. Thereafter, every few months, I would hear from her inquiring whether or not I was seeing anyone. Even if I was not seeing anyone, I always told her that I was. Eventually she got the hint and stopped calling.

Conclusion: There are some girls who you will never be able to figure out. I could never figure out what Jennifer was up to or what she wanted from me. Maybe she didn't even know herself. In any event, it did not matter, as you can't build a relationship on a flimsy, or non-existent, foundation. In retrospect, I should have just kept on driving.

Audrey: The Teutonic Beauty

I met Audrey at a local tennis center where we both played. I think that I fell in love with her the moment that I saw her. She was blonde with a beautiful face and athletic figure. She was also quick-witted, and we began bantering from the moment we met—a big turn-on.

She was very close to her parents and was living with them for the summer before she began her Master's degree

71

at Harvard (of all places), so I got to know her parents very well. They were both from Germany, grew up during the war, and still had much of the old country in their veins. They spoke German for the most part and spoke fondly of all things German. But they went out of their way to be nice to Audrey's new Jewish boyfriend—guilt from the war and all, I assume.

Audrey had just returned from a trip to Italy and was anxious to show me her pictures from the trip, but her mother tried to stop her, and they began having words in another room in both German and English. I couldn't follow the whole conversation, but I was able to ascertain that Audrey's mother objected to showing me the pictures as they contained images of Audrey's "other boyfriend"— that much I could follow. My hopes were dashed. However, I faked a smile while leafing through the photo album. As stated, my dreams and desires for a relationship with Audrey were over. Sad, but true.

In thinking about my relationship with Audrey, I also remember that, while making out, she would always kiss me with a closed mouth. No exceptions. That fact alone should have given me a hint as to how the relationship was going, but I was too blinded by her beauty to see clearly. I wonder how she kissed her other boyfriends. No, actually, I don't wonder about it.

Conclusion: Audrey was a world traveler, and in retrospect, I think that Audrey probably had a boyfriend in every port—something that I could only aspire to. In any event, it would have been hard to land her and still harder to keep her. At the time, the world was her oyster, and I was just a very small part of it. I went away quietly and left her to her other boyfriends. I don't think I was missed, but to be honest, she was definitely missed.

Ariane: The French Client

One of the cardinal rules of being an attorney is that you should never, ever go to bed with a client. But *mon dieu!* Ariane was a pretty French girl with an accent that could melt butter. I was working with her during the day on establishing a business. I was working with her at night on other matters—that is, until one of my law partners strongly suggested that I cease and desist (legal jargon) immediately, which I did. Ariane understood, and we developed a platonic friendship and continued our attorney-client relationship. It could have gone a lot worse for me, so you may well conclude that I dodged the proverbial Gallic bullet.

Conclusion: Well, I don't know what it is like in your profession, but if you are an attorney, do not mix business with pleasure. It could get you fired. It could get you disbarred. It could only end badly. Save yourself the worry and aggravation. Just say *non* to all Gallic and non-Gallic clients alike.

Jodi and the Bahamian Bodybuilder

Her name was Jodi, and she was one of the most beautiful girls that I have ever seen. Have I said that before? Yes, I'm sure that I have, and I will be saying it one more time before this journey ends (see chapter nine—"Jo: Tasmania and The Aussie Dancer").

In any event, I was at a street festival in Denver with my friend Koni (pronounced "Connie"), a beautiful woman in her own right and a platonic friend of mine for years. I spotted Jodi and couldn't take my eyes off of her. I wasn't alone. I was fascinated by the reactions she got from other guys. Men would cross the street to get a better look. Other men were actually barking at her (like dogs—although pigs might be more applicable). As for me, I was too terrified to approach her. Soon, Jodi and her friends went into a bar. Koni talked me into following them into the bar with the words, "Leave it to me." Okay. We saw her at the bar, and Koni struck up a conversation with her and introduced her to me. Simple. Now it was my turn.

Jodi turned out to be as nice as she was beautiful. She was also intelligent. She was in the mortgage business and was also a part-time bodybuilder. She was not muscle-bound, but she was certainly muscle-perfect. That combined with her perfect face, hair, eyes, legs—you get the picture. After conversing for quite some time, we exchanged information—she lived in Calabasas, California—and promised each other that we would keep in touch, and we did. We phoned and corresponded almost daily, and I felt things were going very well. I tried to do cute and clever things for her. For instance, she came down with a bad cold, so I sent a "care package" to her via Federal Express with cold medicines, tea, crackers, etc. Cute, huh? She was thrilled, and I was quite proud of myself. All systems go.

Finally, after a couple of months, we decided that I would fly to LA to see her. In retrospect, that was a big mistake, as I should have met her on my own turf, not hers. She picked me up at LAX, and I could tell right away that the weekend would not go as well as I had hoped. I was charming and funny and gregarious—a veritable Noel

Coward (a veritable *straight* Noel Coward)—but she just seemed disappointed for some reason.

It turns out that it wasn't me at all; she was still carrying a torch for an old boyfriend. That weekend, I heard much more about him than I felt totally necessary. He was a three-hundred-pound, full-time bodybuilder from the Bahamas named Victor. Well, if Victor was her type, what could a one hundred forty-five pound, skinny Jewish attorney do? Nothing, as it turns out. We spent a pleasant few days together, but as in the Fred Astaire song, "A Fine Romance," there were no kisses and no clinches, all because of Victor—at least I like to think so.

I returned to Denver. The relationship, if it could even be called that, was over. I'm sure that Victor got a phone call soon afterward, but not from me.

Conclusion: Well, I think I handled this one as well as could be expected, but if I had to do it all over again, I would have flown her out to Denver—my turf. It may not have made any difference, but it couldn't have hurt. Sometimes you have to take chances. Again, no regrets.

Pam: The Temple and the Police

I had been invited to a singles event on a Saturday night at a local temple. Having no other plans, I decided to go—the height of desperation. However, before I went in, registered, and paid my money, I waited at the front door to see the type of women who would be attending. After a half an hour, I was about to leave, as no one struck my fancy (which can be painful, I hear).

But wait: a very attractive blonde with great legs just

arrived—definitely worth checking out. I went in and immediately began to strike up a conversation with her.

Her name was Pam. She was pretty, bright, interesting, intelligent, and had great legs. Sorry, I already mentioned that.

The party was a bore for both of us, so we explored all off-limits areas of the temple by ourselves. In the process, we began making out in every dark and empty corner of the temple—shades of my bar mitzvah many years before.

Ultimately, we decided to leave the temple party. We hopped into her car for a drive to a local park to take a walk. Unfortunately (or fortunately, depending on how you look at it), we never left the car. We began making out in the front seat and progressed to making love in the back seat.

Suddenly, I saw a bright light shining on the car from about two blocks away. You guessed it: the police. I have never gotten dressed so fast in my life. We were both in presentable condition by the time that the two police officers arrived. They were friendly and understanding, but had been receiving complaints from the neighborhood concerning such practices. At one point, I asked them whether they were going to arrest me for "breaking and entering." I thought that that remark was hilarious. Fortunately, both Pam and police officers shared my sense of humor, and the officers let us off with a warning to "take it indoors next time."

Pam and I thought the entire event was tremendously funny from beginning to end. We saw each other a few more times. She was a great girl, but ultimately, we just drifted apart. I regret not having maintained contact with her, but I never will forget her and our encounter with the men in blue.

Conclusion: Okay … okay … I know. Get a room!

Diana: The Giantess

I was having a business lunch with my partner, Curtis, and we both noticed a beautiful girl at the next table—a veritable Barbie doll. We finished eating and left the restaurant. On the way back to the office, all we could talk about was that girl's beauty. Brave soul that I was, I decided to go back to the restaurant and meet her.

I drove back to the restaurant, and she and her two co-workers were still eating. I made up a lame excuse that I had lost my wallet at the table. One thing led to another, and the group invited me to join them. Wow—just like in the movies.

I got to know all three, but Diana in particular was very sweet, and we seemed to hit it off quite well. She gave me her phone number toward the end of the meal. Then her party got ready to leave. We both stood up to shake hands, and it was then that we both realized that she was fully a foot taller than me. She was as tall as any woman I had ever met. I felt the blood drain from my body in embarrassment. Thankfully, she didn't say anything, but we were both thinking the same thing: alas, it was not meant to be. At least Curtis was impressed that I had been able to obtain her telephone number.

Conclusion: Well, I handled this one as well as could be expected. I was proud of myself for having the nerve to go back to the restaurant and actually meet her. I could have never guessed at the height difference. Nothing ventured, nothing gained. I just wish that she had been a little shorter, or that I had been a lot taller.

Chapter Nine: Foreign Affairs

Spartacus: The Matchmaker

I have always been a great admirer of Kirk Douglas. What other actor could play both Spartacus and Vincent Van Gogh with equal conviction? I have read with interest each of his four volumes of memoirs. As I was reading volume two, *Climbing the Mountain: My Search for Meaning*, a few years ago (a much loftier goal than my search for women), I noticed that he mentioned his editor, Ushi, a great deal.

Apparently, Ushi was a good Catholic girl who had converted to Judaism (as mentioned earlier, Kirk is a devout Jew) and moved to Israel. In the book, there were also some pictures of Ushi, and I thought that she was the cutest little editor that I ever did see. So, you guessed it, I wrote a nice letter to Kirk, sent him a photo, and asked him if he thought Ushi would like to meet a nice Jewish attorney. To my surprise, he responded. He told me that he had forwarded my letter and photo to Ushi, that she was a great girl, very Orthodox (a warning?), and that she was living in Jerusalem. He also gave me her e-mail address.

Of course, I wrote to her right away. We did correspond via e-mail for a month or two. I found her to be very sweet and quite intelligent—just as Kirk had described her in his book. She did mention that Kirk was about to visit her in Jerusalem, and it seemed to me at the time that she was suggesting that I visit her as well. Then she asked me the 64,000-shekel question: "How observant of a Jew are you?" Well, I couldn't lie. I told her that I was not very religious. I think that my exact words were "spiritual" and "hopeful agnostic." It was the kiss of death. I never heard from her after that. However, I recently completed reading the fourth and final volume of Kirk's memoirs. In it, he stated that Ushi had married a rabbi, so I e-mailed her again, and she confirmed that she had indeed married a rabbi in the Israeli Army, and that she had two step-grandchildren. Oh my. *Mazel Tov*! And, belated thanks to Kirk for being so kind.

Conclusion: Well, it never hurts to do semi-outrageous things in the quest for true love. Who knows? It might have worked out, and I could have gotten married in Jerusalem with Spartacus as my best man. Now, that would have been something.

Dr. Cathy: Thailand and the Scottish Doctor

Her name was, and probably still is, Dr. Catherine Watson B_____—very Scottish, with an irresistible Scottish lilt to her voice. We met in Thailand.

Well ... let's start at the beginning. I was sponsoring an adorable young Thai girl named Poj-jana near Khon Kaen, Thailand, under one or another foster-parents' plans. I decided that I would like to visit her, so I signed up with a British tour company for a two-week tour of Thailand. The third week I would spend, on my own, traveling to and meeting with my foster child.

During the "get-acquainted" initial meeting of all tour

members, I noticed a very sweet-looking girl. She had short, dark hair, uneven bangs, a sweet smile, lovely voice, and great legs. Other than that, she was rather ordinary-looking, but she was the best-looking girl in our tour group—similar in nature to the previously described best-looking girl on the first day of class (see chapter 4). But she was sitting next to and talking with an English guy. What was the situation? Were they together? Just my luck. Or was she available?

Later I found out that she had just met him, so she was available. I began to pay more attention to her, and slowly, but surely, I got to know her (actually, not so slowly, but definitely surely). So began an intense mutual flirtation. On one of the first nights of the tour, we were all supposed to get together and meet in the lobby of the hotel at a certain time. I told her that I would stop by her room to pick her up. She was running late and greeted me wearing nothing but a towel. Okay, I'm easy ... I became instantly infatuated.

Each day we spent more and more time together touring through the beautiful country of Thailand. On about day four, I had eaten a rather large Thai meal, had not hydrated sufficiently, and literally passed out while touring the summer palace north of Bangkok. Later, I was told that I was rushed to a hospital in the Polish ambassador's limo—apparently he had been touring the summer palace at the same time. What I do remember is that I asked my Scottish doctor, Cathy, to accompany me to the hospital. The rest of the tour members went off without us.

After an IV or two at the hospital, I was feeling refreshed, and Cathy and I returned to "our" hotel room, alone at last. Cathy had her own room. I, on the other hand, had been rooming with an elderly gentleman from Mauritius. But now I was in Cathy's room to stay—a definite improvement in living arrangements. I recovered quite sufficiently, as we made love all afternoon, before our fellow tour members arrived back. We joined them for dinner, and neither of us could wipe the smiles off of our faces. The next week and a half was right out of the best romance novels. I felt like Fabio! We toured the width and breadth of beautiful Thailand, making love all along the way. Looking back on it, that time with Cathy in Thailand still contains some of the most romantic moments of my life. Wow!

All good things must come to an end, and the two weeks passed all too quickly. Cathy continued on the tour to explore Malaysia while I took off on my own, heading for Khon Kaen. That first night without her was one of the most miserable experiences of my life. Here I had finally found my soulmate, and now she was gone. Forever? I feared so.

Ultimately, I returned to my law practice in Denver, and she returned to her medical practice in London. What to do? We communicated for nine months or so before it was decided that I would fly to London to see her. My plans were to take her to a fancy restaurant and ask her to marry me. The best laid plans ... and boy did these plans go awry!

I remember getting off the plane at Gatwick Airport and picking up my luggage, all the while expecting to see my dear Cathy run into my arms with tears of joy in her eyes. I waited and waited ... and waited. You guessed it. I flew to London for my big date and got stood up. I was devastated.

I booked a room at a hotel on Oxford Street, called the hospital that Cathy worked at and was informed that she had high-tailed it back to Galashiels, Scotland, her hometown. I guess she got cold feet. She was no female Braveheart, that's for sure. At about 3:00 a.m. that first night, I composed my best poison-pen letter and mailed it right away, just in case I changed my mind later on. What a great letter—I wish that I had kept a copy. However, in retrospect, I think that it is all right to write such letters, but you should never, ever actually mail them.

What was a guy to do? I guess that I could have gone to Scotland to retrieve her like John Wayne in *The Quiet Man*. Instead, here I was, all alone in beautiful downtown London. I took advantage of my time in England and spent the next week touring London and taking day trips out of London. I loved it, but it was not exactly the trip that I had expected. To this day, I've still never been to Scotland. Maybe someday. Maybe not. In fact, the sound of bagpipes still leaves a bad taste in my mouth, not to mention my ears.

I later learned via the Internet that she had moved to Glasgow, Scotland. I wrote to her, but never received a response. Sometimes I wonder, what were her reasons? How could she do something like that to me? I suppose it takes all kinds in this world, and to speculate would be a complete waste of time. Although, I must admit that I have wasted time in such speculation. In the end, it was a great adventure—both Thailand and London. It could have been worse.

Conclusion: As I have stated before, a holiday romance is never based in reality, no matter how intense or real it seems at the time. Trust me. If you find yourself in a holiday romance, enjoy it for all it's worth, but do not take it too seriously once you arrive home. Holiday memories are great, but home is reality, and the two can never be reconciled. And, if you like to travel like me, always keep that in mind.

Afterthought on Thailand: Thailand is a beautiful country, and the people are warm and friendly. Thailand is called "The Land of Smiles," and for good reason.

The Thais take their Buddhist religion very seriously. In fact, it is a crime to take a figure of Buddha out of the country. Of course, that doesn't stop every street vendor from selling them to unsuspecting tourists. In addition, the Thais consider the feet as unclean. For example, it is impolite to point with your feet.

Well, as I was going through customs on my way back from Bangkok to Denver, a customs inspector discovered a Buddha head in my luggage. Alarms went off, and the chief customs inspector arrived—a very stern woman lacking anything that could be called a "smile." I knew that I was really in trouble when it was discovered that I had wrapped the Buddha head in my socks. I was taken away for interrogation. After much apologizing and kowtowing, I was free to go, *sans* one Buddha head. Of course, upon my arrival in Denver, my luggage was nowhere to be found. It took three weeks to finally track it down and retrieve it. I guess that I was being taught a lesson, one you should remember if you ever venture forth to Thailand.

Jo: Tasmania and the Aussie Dancer

She was one of the most beautiful girls that I have ever seen. I know, I know. Not again, you say. As promised earlier, this is the absolute last time that I will say it.

I had just taken a two-week tour of Australia, where I found the Aussie girls to be beautiful, friendly, and quite approachable. Now I was exploring Tasmania on my own for a few days. In case some of you don't know, Tasmania is one of the states in Australia. It is the island just south of the Australian mainland, and it is like taking a trip back in time to Jane Austen's England: beautiful and quaint. Hobart is the capital and main port city of Tasmania, and for all you trivia buffs, it was the birthplace of Errol Flynn (another hero of mine for dubious reasons).

I was walking among the shops and restaurants along the pier in Hobart, and suddenly I found myself face to face with "a perfect ten." She had a perfect face, a perfect smile, and a perfect dancer's body. I knew that I had to get to know her.

Before I proceed, please note that I have not used a numbering system to describe any of the women detailed in this book. First, I find it demeaning and sexist. (Yes, even I think so.) Second, I find the terms not very useful. I have noticed, however, that "perfect tens" tend to be friendlier, more sincere, and more approachable than sevens, eights, or nines. Those women sometimes have a chip on their shoulder, as they are not tens and tend to be more self-absorbed and less friendly to men. That's just my observation.

Back to our story … where were we? Oh yes, I just had to get to know her. Being a brave soul, I went up to her and started talking to her. She was delightful and very friendly. Her name was Jo, and she was a dancer with the Sydney Dance Company. They were just completing a tour of Australia, and that night was their final performance in the small theatre (as the Aussies spell it) in Hobart. One thing led to another, and we arranged to meet after the performance for a drink. Perfect.

Yes, perfect, except, oh no, I had just completed almost three weeks of touring Australia, and I didn't have an appropriate outfit to wear to the theatre. No problem. I had all afternoon to shop in Hobart for a decent outfit. Big problem. Hobart is a lovely city, but there were no quality men's clothing stores in the entire city. At least I didn't find any. I did the best I could—nice shirt, black vest, new denim jeans (I know, I know, but it was the best I could do).

I put my new outfit on, bought a dozen long-stemmed red roses, and made my way to the theatre, feeling very much like William Holden. I asked one of the attendants to deliver the flowers backstage to "my friend, Jo." He asked, "What's her last name?" I confessed that I did not know. He responded, "She must be a close friend." Everyone is a comedian ... but the flowers were delivered.

After the performance, which was a series of modern/jazz dances in which she was quite good, but, not great, I went backstage and searched for her. Time went by, the theatre emptied, and I still couldn't find her. Oh no! Finally, I saw her in the dressing room, all alone. She had been waiting for me and thought that I had stood her up. Not a chance.

We had a delightful after-performance snack of champagne and dessert, accompanied by a delightful conversation. Sadly, my dream date ended all too quickly. We exchanged information and did correspond fitfully for about six months or so. Later, she advised me that she had accepted a job dancing in Amsterdam and that she would contact me from there. I was curious as to what type of dancing she would be doing in Amsterdam, but I never got to find out, as I never heard from her again. So, Jo, if you ever read this tome, I would love to hear from you.

Conclusion: See the conclusion after Dr. Cathy: Thailand and the Scottish Doctor. Was this really a holiday romance or just a fun first-meeting story? Probably a bit of both. Still the fates and the probabilities were against it. Sometimes you just have to go for it, regardless of the ultimate outcome. No regrets. Okay, maybe just one regret—that I did not move to Amsterdam.

Vanda: San Diego and the Russian Model

I have met them in all different ways, but this one was an exceptional meeting, even for me. I had signed up with an international pen-pal service whereby you could correspond with women from all over the world. (Desperation? You bet.) This particular service featured women primarily from countries of the former Soviet Union and from Asia. I had dated Russian and Asian women before and had enjoyed dating many, but not all, of them. There is something intriguing about foreign women, at least for me.

Through this service I met Vanda, a fashion model living in Moscow. I saw her photo in the "girl catalog," wrote her a nice letter enclosing a photo of myself, and received a sweet letter and some beautiful photos in return. The Internet was in its infancy at the time, so we corresponded mostly by regular mail and fax.

Vanda seemed like a very sweet girl, and those photos … be still my heart! She was incredibly sexy and gorgeous. Where was this going to lead? I was not about to fly to

Moscow to meet her. (You will recall my experience in London with, I mean without, Dr. Cathy.) Then Vanda mentioned that she would be in San Diego for a photo shoot and would I meet her there? Would I? You bet! And just in case ... I had never been to San Diego so I would enjoy exploring there by myself if it came to that.

I booked myself a room at a downtown hotel, rented a car, and waited for her call. Thankfully, the call came. We arranged to have dinner that night. I picked her up where she was staying, and we had a lovely dinner. Yes, it was the same person that I had been corresponding with. And yes, she most definitely had to be a model. She was amazing.

We spent a few days together, but like many Russian women that I have known, she had a very dour personality. Picture Natasha of Boris and Natasha/Bullwinkle fame. What I couldn't get over was her lack of enthusiasm for her surroundings. I was so impressed: the Pacific Ocean, the Gaslamp Quarter, Coronado Island, etc. I kept asking her if she liked this or that aspect of San Diego, and it was always, "*Nyet! Nyet!*" She was from dank Moscow and was not at all impressed with gorgeous San Diego? What was wrong with her?

I eventually found out what was wrong. One night I was driving her back from a lovely dinner at Croce's (shameless plug), and we saw a limousine that was literally two blocks long—the longest limo I had ever seen. Vanda looked at me and said, "That is first thing I see in United States I am impressed" (her exact words—accent and all). From that point on, I knew this relationship had no hope. How do you spell "shallow" in Russian? *V-A-N-D-A*. She was ten times more shallow than I was.

Our time was up, and we parted amiably, never to

see each other again. I would occasionally see her on various international pen-pal Web sites, but I never did communicate with her again. In the end, I hope that she found all the stretch limos that her heart desired.

Conclusion: You pays your money (or rubles) and you takes your chances. No regrets. And I did truly enjoy beautiful San Diego, despite Vanda. If you are ever in a similar situation, just relax and enjoy your surroundings, even if that enjoyment is not shared by your companion. If she is a model from Moscow, you can bet that that enjoyment will not be shared.

Montreal and the Nameless Indonesian Girl

The same international pen-pal service and, basically, the same result—this correspondent was a pretty girl from Indonesia, and even though we corresponded for some months, her name escapes me.

In any event, she was planning a trip to visit relatives in Montreal and asked if I would join her for a few days. I had never been to Montreal, so you guessed it. Montreal was not a disappointment in the least. Unfortunately, I can't say the same thing about the rest of the trip.

We had planned to meet in one of the shopping centers in downtown Montreal, and we did, but from the moment we met, we both knew that there was absolutely no chemistry between us. We tried to have a pleasant time for a few days, but I'm sure that we were both counting the hours until I had to leave Montreal and return to work. Obviously, we did not stay in touch, but I loved Montreal. However, falling in love with a city is never quite as satisfying as falling in love with a girl. As you can tell by now, I've had ample experience at both.

Conclusion: There must be mutual chemistry for a relationship to flourish. If there is no "spark," there will be no flame, and flame is a good thing, as Martha Stewart might say.

Alexandra Hartman:
The Aussie Girl Who Did Not Exist

Same international dating site; different result. She said her name was Alexandra Hartman from Perth, Australia. I am using a last name just this one time for reasons that will soon become all too obvious. She had drop-dead gorgeous pictures. She said she was a medical student. She said that her father, Dr. Alex Hartman, was a noted surgeon who had recently died. And Alexandra seemed to like me a lot. In fact, from the very start, she seemed to like me almost too much to be believed—a clear warning sign.

By the way, have you ever had international phone sex? Believe me, it can get expensive—but it can be fun. I must give her credit. Besides that, she was also a gifted conversationalist. She was incredibly knowledgeable about many topics like history, art, politics, movies, and so on. At least she talked a good game.

As with anything in life, if it sounds too good to be true, it is. Eventually I got suspicious as Alexandra just sounded too good to be true. She was always vague about making plans to get together, and she just seemed to have entirely too much time on her hands to be a medical student.

I decided to engage a private detective in Perth, which was far easier and less expensive than you might guess. I discovered that there had never been a Dr. Alex Hartman, dead or alive, and that there was no Alexandra Hartman registered in any of the local medical schools. In fact, there was no Alexandra Hartman, at all. However, she had given me her address—a home, I found out, that was owned and occupied by a Mr. Victor and Mrs. Yvonne K_____. Armed with such knowledge, I was able to catch her in many lies. I never confronted her with the truth, as it really didn't matter by then. Apparently, Yvonne was (and probably still is) a bored and lonely housewife who gets her jollies by impersonating a beautiful Aussie girl for the attention that it brings her. Sad really, but I guess everyone must have a hobby.

Conclusion: As I previously stated … and this goes for anything in life, including women: if it sounds too good to be true, it is. Just walk away.

Chapter Ten: Match.com
and Other Disasters

My dad and I once speculated on the number of women that I have gone out with since first attending college at the age of eighteen. We concluded that the number was in the high hundreds. That number may seem inflated to you, but consider the fact that I have never been married, I have dated a lot of women, I am in my fifties, and this number includes not only past relationships, but also those women whom I might have met for coffee for a half-hour and would never see again. There have been quite a number of those latter type of dates. Any comparisons to Wilt Chamberlain would be completely erroneous on your part.

Frankly, some of those one-date affairs have been more interesting and/or humorous than the others. Let's just say more humorous than interesting.

As I state in the next chapter, Match.com is not a bad way to meet women, but I think that you will find that most "Match dates" will be one-date adventures. But that rule applies to most dates, no matter how you meet them. The following is just a sampling of some of those dating disasters, both non-Match and Match. Many of them were one-date disasters, but I have also included a few multi-date girls whose stories ended just as disastrously.

Perhaps "disaster" is too strong a term. You'll find neither the Hindenburg crash nor the Battle of Stalingrad described here, but, in Barry World, these stories would be considered disasters.

Diane and the Car Door

This one was a fix-up. In retrospect, it was a fix-up by someone who clearly did not have my best interests at heart. Anyway, Diane and I arranged to have dinner, and she wanted to pick me up to show off her new Honda Accord. The car was nice and the dinner was fine, so I called her a few days later, and she let loose with an invective the likes of which I had never heard. Apparently, I had closed her car door a bit too roughly—"slammed" was the word she used—and she was incensed. I was just confused as I didn't recall treating her car door with anything but the greatest respect. In any event, I was shocked at her reaction. I was also relieved to have gotten to know the real Diane right at the beginning so as to not waste any more time with her.

Joan and Her CDs

Joan was actually a very nice, professional woman. She had invited me over for a home-cooked meal, which all bachelors appreciate. The dinner and the company were fine. Then I volunteered to help her clean up the kitchen. (Mom did not raise a rube.) As I went to load her dishwasher, I noticed that her compact discs were neatly lined up inside. I asked her about it, and she stated that that was how she cleaned her CDs. I was appalled. As you can probably tell by now, I am a bit anal-compulsive, and I take good care of my CDs. Putting them in the dishwasher … that was beyond the pale. I simply couldn't get over it and never did call Joan back for a second date.

Rachel the Stripper

I was walking to the swimming pool in my old townhome complex when suddenly I saw a vision of loveliness sitting on a balcony and talking on the phone. She was a beautiful brunette with a lovely figure and gorgeous tanned legs. As she was on the phone, I slipped her my business card, having written on the back, "Call me—I have a million questions to ask you." She called the next day. Wow. This could be the start of something big (an old song by Steve Allen, I believe).

The next week we had dinner, and she was delightful. She was a big improvement over Emily the stripper, who I had not yet met (see chapter seven). Her name was Rachel, and she was an exotic dancer at one of the higher-end "gentlemen's clubs" in town. I was proud to say that I had never been there (and still haven't), but I didn't hold it against her. She was very bright. She said that she would "perform" for two years and save all her money for college. I was impressed.

After dinner, I asked her back to my place. She declined and said she would rather sit on her balcony and talk. We did so for a few minutes until we were interrupted by a tall, muscular fellow without a neck who demanded to know who I was. I asked him the same question—I was braver back then. Well, as it turns out, he was her long-standing boyfriend, and Rachel knew he would be arriving around that time. I had been cruelly used. She used her date with an attorney to make her Neanderthal boyfriend jealous, and it worked. I left before things got out of hand with life and limb (mine) intact. It was disappointing, but not totally unexpected. I never saw hide nor hair of her again.

Sunny, Kim, and the Korean Switch

I met two beautiful Korean roommates who both worked at a local sushi restaurant. I liked them both right away. Sunny was tall and thin with beautiful long, black hair and a thick Korean accent. Kim was shorter with dark hair and no trace of a Korean accent—much more Americanized. For some reason, I asked out Sunny first, and we had a few dates, but it wasn't clicking into place for me. I decided that I would prefer to date Kim. The problem … how to effect "The Switch"—stop dating one roommate and start dating another? Well, I called Kim and arranged for a date, and we did meet for dinner. However, throughout dinner, she just kept emphasizing to me what a great girl she thought Sunny was. Unfortunately, Kim was more interested in getting me back with Sunny than getting involved with me herself. We parted friends, but I never called Sunny back. It obviously went nowhere with Kim. For once in my life, I had attempted the switch and failed utterly. Oh, well—again, nothing ventured, nothing gained.

Lisa, a.k.a. Hulk Hogan

It started out well. We met at an art gallery, and apparently, she enjoyed the fine arts as much as I did. Her name was Lisa. She was from Alabama and had the cutest Southern accent. As I picked her up for our first date, she presented me with a flower. How sweet. Nothing could go wrong with this one, right? Wrong. I made the mistake of sleeping with her, and to put it mildly, she liked things rough. I, on the other hand, like things a bit more gentle—just a personal preference. When we were done, I distinctly remember going into the bathroom to check my body for scratches and bruises. I felt like I had just gone ten rounds with Mike Tyson. After that encounter, I reluctantly made the unilateral decision that that relationship was over.

Dana and Talking Dirty

Another sweet girl. And again, a flower. And again, I ended up in bed with her. Things seemed to be going well. Then she started using some off-color words. That experience was new to me at the time, but I decided to join in the verbal fun, or at least just try to keep up my end of the conversation. So I threw out a few words of my own— very few. She became furious and was quite offended. She reminded me that she was "a lady" (what did that make me?), and that I should have had more respect for her. She left in a huff (or "a minute and a huff," as Groucho might say), and I never saw her again. In retrospect, I think she was just a bit crazy. And again, good riddance.

Cynthia the Fashion Disaster

She was wonderful in so many ways: a blue-eyed blonde with a lovely figure and sweet disposition, but—and I couldn't get over it—she was a complete fashion disaster. Her fashion sense was nonexistent, and it drove me crazy. Now, I am no Beau Brummell, but I do have a modicum of fashion sense, and I really appreciate a girl who knows how to dress well. I guess the attempted relationship with Cynthia was a non-starter to begin with. Perhaps I should have just taken her shopping. Perhaps daily. About a year after I stopped seeing her, my girlfriend *du jour* and I ran into her at the mall. There had been no improvement in her appearance. I think any attempted styling on my part would have been fruitless. Shallow on my part, I admit it, but … such a waste.

Kristi the Swing Dancer

Kristi was a Match.com disaster, as are all of the date descriptions that follow. She was an attractive brunette. We met for lunch and had a nice time, so we decided to take swing-dance lessons together. Later in the week, we met at the dance hall, and I paid for a month of lessons for the both of us, consisting of one lesson a week. I was terrible, but I thought we had a nice time. Well, as you can guess, I showed up the next week, and Kristi was nowhere to be seen—no phone call, no e-mail, nothing. Well, *I* enjoyed the last three lessons. I didn't improve much, but it was fun. And I learned everything about Kristi that I needed to know.

Lydia the Aussie "Hottie"

One of my pet peeves is when a girl refers to herself as "hot" or a "hottie." Well, Lydia did both. We were on our first (and only) date, and to be fair, she was a nice girl and did bear a passing resemblance to Jennifer Aniston—just a passing resemblance, mind you. But she kept referring to herself as "hot." It was not only a turn-off, but I didn't have the heart to tell her that she wasn't all that hot. Oh, well. We never saw each other again. I am sure that some other guy thought that she was, indeed, hot. Good luck to both of them.

Ashley and the Doggy Bag

Another pet peeve of mine is a dinner date who orders way too much food and packs it all into doggy bags to feast on for the next few days. Ashley was even worse. She ordered an expensive dessert to go. She did not order it for herself, but explained to me that she was bringing it back to her roommate's sons, who she thought would really enjoy it. I bit my tongue, but inside I was seething. How rude. I couldn't wait to get away from her. I hope those sweet young boys got tummy-aches. Sorry, bad attitude.

Olga and Her Cell Phone

There seem to be a lot of Russian immigrants on Match .com. I believe that I know the reason why—free meals and/or the possibility of a green card. Anyway, Olga was a true beauty. We met at a restaurant for dinner, and I could tell right away that I was not her cup of borscht. When that happens to me, I still try to make the evening as pleasant as possible. Olga, on the other hand, spent most of the evening in the restroom—no doubt furiously calling friends on her cell phone, trying to arrange alternative plans. People have since told me that I should have paid the bill and left her. I guess that I was just too much of a gentleman. I waited for her and, mercifully, the evening did not last too long.

Katherine and *Her* Cell Phone

Not too long after my experience with Olga (above), I met Katherine, a pretty girl from Central America. She was not quite my type, but we were having what I thought was a pleasant meal. All of a sudden, she decided to call her young son who was, according to her, visiting relatives in Maryland. Five minutes passed—no Katherine. After ten minutes, our waiter asked me whether or not she had left. I told him that I didn't think so, but after fifteen minutes (and with thoughts of Olga in my head), I paid the check and left—half-expecting to run into her at the restaurant entrance. Nope. I never saw her again. For all I know, she may still be there, or, had it not been for my experience with Olga, I may have still been there.

Kristen the Talker

I knew that I was in trouble during our first phone conversation when I could not get a single word in edgewise—not one word. Finally I called my home phone from my cell phone, informed her that I had a call from my mom, and had to get off the phone. My mistake was in agreeing to meet her for dinner. Kristen was late and apologized by planting a wet, sloppy kiss on my lips. As you already know by now, I am no prude, but that is one kiss that I could have done without. Get to know me for at least a few minutes before you kiss me, please! Well, if I thought the face-to-face meeting would go better than the telephone conversation, I was mistaken. I still could not get a word in edgewise. I ate as fast as I could and shot pleading glances at our waitress in the hope that she would hurry up with the check. I got out of there as quickly as humanly possible and with at least most of my sanity intact. Dreadful.

Svetlana and the Kisses

Another Russian girl … well, actually in Svetlana's case, it was Ukrainian. As alluded to above, Russian/Ukrainian girls will always ask to meet at expensive restaurants for dinner, and it is usually the dinners that they are often after, not you. No quick coffee dates for these girls, no way. In any event, Svetlana was cute and seemed rather sweet. Dinner was enjoyable—expensive, but enjoyable. The restaurant was in a nice shoppette, so we went window shopping, started to hold hands, and, yes, even kiss. Well, I thought this one may actually turn into something. Wrong. Later, I called and e-mailed, but never received a response from her and never saw her again. What happened? Well, it was probably the case that she had another date shortly thereafter (maybe even that same day) and that she preferred him to me. Fickle? Yes. Shallow? You bet. I just chalked it up to another bad experience with a daughter of Russia or Ukraine. Maybe I should change my mind and always buy American. Maybe.

Kate the Opera Singer

Kate appeared pretty well perfect. Her pictures were beautiful, her profile was fascinating, and she was an opera singer. What a great match for me: someone who was also very interested in the fine arts, and someone with the talent to actually make a living at it. We carried an

101

e-mail correspondence for a couple of weeks, and I started to become very interested in her. We even began sending flirtatious e-mails. So what happened? Well, we met, and God bless her, but her pictures had to be at least ten years old. And she outweighed me by at least twenty pounds. I felt misled and just a bit used. Apparently, she was not too crazy about me either. But, it was only a quick coffee-date so we were both very cordial knowing that our date would soon be over. No harm, no foul.

Chapter Eleven: Dating Services That I Have Known

Great Expectations

Great Expectations is a video-dating service. I tend to view this service as one of low expectations. They have very attractive and slick saleswomen and they talk a good game. They even show you pictures of very attractive, "available" women in their system. As it turns out, many of these women are "on freeze," meaning that they are not available.

My experience has been that I have rejected most of the women that have chosen me and vice-versa. Could that old Groucho line come into play here? "I would never join any club that would have me as a member."

To be fair, I have had two very good female friends who have met their husbands through Great Expectations, so there you have it.

It's Just Lunch

This service interviews you and then fixes you up with other members, sight unseen, for lunch. Again, they have an attractive and slick sales staff who practically gush that they have so many of the type of women that you are looking for. After a few lunch dates, I became convinced that they don't really listen or try to match you appropriately. They just try to match you as quickly as possible so that, hopefully, you will re-sign with them. I had a number of conversations with my representative, but all to no avail. I finally gave up before my membership was over.

Eight Minute Dating

There are a number of "speed-dating" services, but I think this one is the best known. It's not bad, really. You meet eight different people over eight minutes, and then, the next day, you log onto their site and choose the ones in whom you are interested. If they also choose you, you get their names and phone numbers.

It's a cute idea, and I've been to about a half dozen of their events. However, I have not had too much success with this service. Don't ask my why. Perhaps I shall try it again.

eHarmony

Well, you all have heard their ads on radio and TV, and it sounds great. You fill out an online form, which takes about forty-five minutes, you submit it and pay a fee, and then they fix you up with your "soulmate." Unfortunately, I did not get past their online survey. After I concluded it, I was advised that they could not help me. Do you think that they can diagnose "shallow" online?

I actually know many people who have been rejected. The one woman I talked to who wasn't rejected stated that she wasn't all that thrilled with their matching process. But … I never got a chance to find out for myself.

Match.com

Well, so far, this has been the best service for me. You post your photos and profile online and connect with others who have done the same. The site is most like the real dating world, and you get the good, the bad, and the ugly. Some photos are old and some profiles are dishonest, but for the most part, it is a pretty good and pretty inexpensive way to jump into the world of online dating. Hopefully, the following is a helpful hint: once you have met someone on line, do not spend an inordinate amount of time exchanging e-mails or engaging in telephone conversations. You may be wasting a whole lot of time and getting yourself worked up for nothing. Meeting is key, so once you've connected on line, arrange to meet right away. Then, if it doesn't work out, you haven't wasted a lot of time or mental energy.

Meetup.com

In many cities such as San Diego, there is a city-specific Web site called Meetup.com. Here you can search for groups with specific interests and meet others with those same interests. Whether you like to bike or hike or wish to learn Chinese or swing dance, there will probably be a group for you to join to meet like-minded individuals and maybe even like-minded women.

Cherry Blossoms

This one is an international Internet dating service featuring mostly women from Asian countries and countries of the former Soviet Union. It is inexpensive—a one-time fee per year—and there are thousands of women to choose from. I guess the idea is that you connect by e-mail, arrange to visit her, and if you get along, fly her to the United States on a fiancée visa. I have never taken it nearly that far, but have corresponded with many women. This site is how I met Vanda and how I *didn't* meet Alexandra (see chapter nine). Beware: there are numerous scammers (those who are looking for money) and spammers (those who steer you to other paying sites, such as translation services). Just be careful and be smart. If a girl falls in love with you after the first few e-mails, run away fast.

Anastasia

Another international Internet dating site focusing on Russian and Ukrainian women, and there are thousands of pictures of beautiful women. It is an expensive site, as you are charged for each e-mail sent and received, and that can add up to big bucks.

I also question whether all the women on this site are genuine. For example, I was writing to one woman for a while and then quit the site. A few months later, I rejoined, and she was still on the site. So I wrote to her again and when she answered, it was just as if I had never corresponded with her. She didn't seem to know who I was. Either she had a very bad memory (unlikely), or her picture was being used by someone to elicit a steady stream of e-mails (or horror of horrors, could it have been a fat, naked man in his basement in Moscow?). You decide. To be fair, Anastasia has one of the better reputations for this type of business, so they must be doing something right.

Chapter Twelve: Some Conclusions on Life, Liberty, and the Pursuit of Women

What have I learned after all of this? Precious little, I suspect, but in addition to the conclusion at the end of each story above, there are certain other rules (a few repeated for emphasis) that I now try to live by—as follows:

1. Always pick Mary Ann.

2. Always pick Tonya.

3. Before approaching any girl, always check the ring finger. If there is a ring there, of any kind, walk away. She is either engaged/married, or she may be wearing it for protection to ward off guys like me. In any event, it is not worth pursuing.

4. First impressions are pretty reliable. I would stick with them. 'Nuff said.

5. Girls generally are not interested in "trading up" (or, in fairness, "trading down"). If you meet a girl, and she is from a vastly different (especially lower) socioeconomic background than you are, odds are that she will not be interested in you. I have encountered this situation a number of times.

Women prefer to date men within their own social "milieu." (I love that word.) That's just the way it is. Don't try to change it. Just accept it as a fact and move on.

6. The grass is never greener. Quit looking over the fence at your neighbor's lawn (or wife). His grass is not greener, no matter what it may look like to you. Cultivate and appreciate the relationship that you have instead of wishing it was something or someone else. The more active you are in looking for greener pastures, the less successful you will be in maintaining a stable and healthy relationship.

7. Don't be like the proverbial kid in the candy store. Don't feel like you have to taste every different kind of candy in the store. If you are enjoying one piece, stick with it. Avoid the tummy-ache. I hope the analogy makes sense to you—it's a pretty easy one to decipher.

8. Never, ever (ever!) date a woman who is married, or even just separated. This conclusion should be a no-brainer, but you would be surprised at how often it is ignored. I have even ignored it once or twice myself. If the relationship was meant to be, it will survive the time it takes to have a divorce granted. (Listen to your attorney!) And if it doesn't so survive, it wasn't a worthwhile relationship to begin with.

9. Conversely, don't *you* date anyone while you are married or in an exclusive relationship. It is a rule many men violate at one time or another. Again,

I am guilty of it myself. But it can only lead to disaster and heartbreak to any number of people.

10. Knowledge gained through experience is costly wisdom. I don't know who first told me that, but think about it. I think it actually has some relevance to the topics at hand.

11. Always take the high road. Always do the honorable thing. You will be surprised at the number of times that this action will *not* be reciprocated, but, do so anyway, as it is the right thing to do. Very important. Please trust me on this one.

12. Do unto others as you would have them do unto you. Always follow The Golden Rule. It has been called "The Golden Rule" for a reason and has been around since at least the time of Confucius. Again, even if not reciprocated, treat her as you would wish to be treated. Also, very important. Please trust me on this one as well!

13. Never, ever take anyone for granted. If you are in a stable and committed relationship, thank your lucky stars. Think every day about what you can do to make her happy—anything from giving her a small gift to taking out the garbage. Make it a conscious effort every single day. I know it is extremely difficult, if not almost impossible. The alternative is the possibility of losing a relationship, which you may regret for the rest of your life.

14. Long-distance relationships never last. I don't care if you are in a different city, state, or country;

ultimately, you will be disappointed. The only exception that I have encountered is in so-called "open relationships," wherein two people lead separate lives, especially sexually. I hear that Shirley MacLaine was married for decades to a husband who resided permanently in Japan. If you actually want to spend time with your significant other, stay within the same geographic area.

15. There is nothing worse than a lost opportunity. If you see someone you are interested in, go for it. Approach her. The worst thing that can happen is that you will be rejected. Big deal. There is a scene in the movie *Citizen Kane* where the Everett Sloane character, as an old man, is describing a beautiful woman he once saw in his youth. Even many years later, he could describe her exactly and was still upset with himself for not attempting to get to know her. I have had many such lost opportunities myself and remember quite a few of them. Make the effort. Sure you may get rejected and feel foolish, but that scenario is better than not making the effort at all.

16. A caveat to Rule fifteen above—don't try to hit on attractive bartenders or flight attendants. These women are bothered by men like me every minute of their working lives. Give them a break. And give yourself a break, as you will, in all probability, be unsuccessful. Don't even consider these women as opportunities that you will regret losing—they are not.

17. Do not become a "Stage Door Johnny." In the olden days, these were men who waited at the stage door of a theater for an actress to appear after a show. In a more modern sense, these are men who are romantically interested in a certain woman, can never get past the friendship stage and wait around hoping for romance. It never, ever happens. All good things do *not* come to those who wait. Once you are slotted in the "friend" category, either accept it or move on.

18. Finally, on a lighter note, we have something in our family called "love presents." These are small gifts that we give for no special occasion other than to say, "I am thinking of you." Give some love presents. I bet that it will make you feel as good as the recipient—it always does for me!

Postscript

As I was writing this book, my dad, Charles Rothman, died. He passed away six days after my parents' fifty-eighth wedding anniversary. Although this book deals with *romantic* relationships, let me say a word about family relationships. Enjoy your relationships with family members while you can, as you never know how long you will be lucky enough to have these people in your life. Don't let petty things get in the way. And don't ever forget to keep saying "I love you." It will do your heart good.

Printed in the United States
150945LV00001B/86/P